# The Rare Jewel of Christian Contentment: Abridged and in Modern English

# The Rare Jewel of Christian Contentment: Abridged and in Modern English

Original text by Jeremiah Burroughs.
First published 1648.

Abridged and reworded by Rob Summers

To Sheila Oliver

# Table of Contents

# Introduction

*The Rare Jewel of Christian Contentment* was written in the 17<sup>th</sup> century by the eminent Puritan preacher Jeremiah Burroughs (1599-1646). It is a wealth of observations, advice, and apt comparisons for the benefit of anyone discontented, that is, for anyone unhappy, depressed, miserable, or upset. Over the centuries many readers have benefited from Burroughs' blend of loving admonishment and encouragement. However, though some people are used to reading works from past eras, most are not. When I have tried to share copies with friends, they have not been able to get past the 17<sup>th</sup> century language.

My friend Debbie, knowing that I am an author of indie novels, suggested that I use my skills to change Burroughs' original text into modern English. That I have done, and I have also abridged the text, reducing it to less than half its former length. That might seem excessive unless you consider that the book consists of the texts of sermons—very good sermons but with all the repetitions you might expect in messages intended to be heard and remembered. Some might say that Burroughs' inclination to repeat himself goes beyond the average even for preachers. At any rate, I feel the abridgement has sacrificed little of what he had to say.

Other changes I have made include organizing the text into shorter paragraphs, dropping out the old-fashioned numbering of headings, and wherever scripture is within quotation marks, substituting text from the *New American Standard Bible*; all to make the book more reader friendly.

Burroughs preached the sermons his book was based on in 1645 during the English Civil War. Though he and his congregation did not know it at the time, the worst of the battles and tumult was over. Soon they would be able to sleep safely in their beds. But in the meantime, his hearers were troubled by fears and worries. Rather than preach soothingly to them, Jeremiah, who knew his people well, chose to challenge them. His text could hardly be summarized as, "You poor, poor things!" but more as, "Live out your faith in Jesus!" It is my hope and prayer that Burroughs' message will continue to be, as he put it in the original, "a very timely cordial to revive the drooping spirits of the saints."

--Rob Summers

**Chapter 1 - A Description of Christian Contentment**

*"...I have learned to be content in whatever circumstances I am"*
*(Philippians 4:11)*

This statement of the Apostle Paul contains a comforting medicine to lift Christians' spirits in these sad and disheartening times. For temptation and trial have come to all of us, a time of tribulation that we feel keenly.

Paul presents us with the heart and soul of practical godly living. We see in his words his proficiency in the 'school of Christ' and what we must learn too if we are to experience the power and growth of godliness in our souls.

In context Paul is trying to persuade the Philippians that he was not the sort to yearn for the great things of this world, and that in fact he did not want anything that belonged to them, though he did want *them*, in the sense of desiring their allegiance to Christ. He did not long for wealth; his heart was given to better things. In effect he says, "I don't mean that I lack anything, for whether I have or go without, I'm fully satisfied and have enough. I've learned to be content in whatever circumstances I am."

When he says he has *learned* this, he indicates that achieving persistent contentment is an art, a spiritual secret: something to be revealed and learned. So in verse 12 he affirms: "I know how to get along with humble means, and I also know how to live in prosperity; in any and every circumstance I have learned the secret..." He is saying that, though he did not know the art of contentment at first,

1

with much effort he achieved it, and now, by the grace of God, he has mastered it.

The word 'content' has a fullness of meaning in the original Greek that is not apparent in translation. In a strict sense its meaning can only be attributed to God, who has called himself 'God all-sufficient,' because he rests fully satisfied in himself alone. But he is pleased to give this fullness to Christians. In this sense Paul can declare himself to have self-sufficiency. This of course does not mean that anyone but God can be self-sufficient, but that Paul has found thorough satisfaction through the grace of Christ. He says, "Though I don't have material comforts and conveniences to supply my necessities, yet Christ supplies my soul with enough to satisfy me plentifully in every situation."

I write with the one goal of calming and comforting Christians during the troubles and changes they meet with in these heart-shaking times. My main point is that being skilled in Christian contentment is the duty, glory, and excellence of a Christian. Other scriptures confirm this. I Timothy 6:8 says that "If we have food and covering, with these we shall be content." There is the duty. Verse 6 of the same passage says, "But godliness actually is a means of great gain when accompanied by contentment." There is the glory and excellence of it (in which Paul suggests that without contentment godliness would not be gain.). Furthermore, Hebrews 13:5 reads, "Make sure that your character is free from the love of money, being content with what you have."

I will try to demonstrate four things in this book: 1. What Christian contentment is, 2. The art and secret of it, 3. What lessons must be learned to bring the heart to contentment, and 4. What the glorious excellence of this grace chiefly consists of.

This is my definition: *Christian contentment is that sweet, inward, quiet, grace-filled condition of spirit which freely submits to and delights in God's wise and fatherly management in every condition.*

I will explain this description word by word, for it is very comforting and useful for troubled people in unsettled times and situations.

2

**Contentment is *inward*. It is a work of the Spirit *indoors*.**

Contentment does not come just by refraining from outward violence, or by holding back from grumbling words and attitudes against God and others. It is the inward submission of the heart. "My soul, wait in silence for God only" (Psalm 62:5). Not only must the tongue be silent, the soul must be too. Many sit silently without complaining while inwardly they are bursting with discontentment. They have agitation and stubbornness in their hearts. Despite their outward silence, God hears the peevish, fretful language of their souls. A shoe may be smooth and trim outside while inside it pinches the skin. Similarly, some may have outward calmness and stillness while within them are confusion, bitterness, disturbance, and vexation.

If gaining true contentment were as easy as keeping quiet outwardly, it would not require much learning. Then it could be had with less strength and skill than an apostle possessed, and even less than an ordinary Christian has. But there is more to contentment than can be achieved just by applying average abilities and reasoning, though those do often restrain us. It is a business of the heart.

**Contentment is the *quiet* of the heart.**

All is sedate and still within. To clarify, I add that this quiet, gracious condition of spirit is not opposed to certain things:

*Contentment is not opposed to feeling our misfortunes*. God allows us to be mindful of what we suffer. Christ does not say, "Do not count as a cross what is a cross." He says, "Take up your cross daily." It is like a patient's reaction to medicine: if you take the dose and vomit it, or if you feel nothing and it does not help you, either way the medicine does no good, but the result suggests that you are seriously ill and desperate for a cure. So it is with our spirits when we are under trial: whether you cannot bear troubles or you are insensitive to them, either way it is a symptom that your soul is in a dangerous and almost incurable condition. There can be no true contentment if you are unconcerned about and insensitive to your hardships.

*Contentment is not opposed to making a reasonable complaint to God, and to our friends*. Though a Christian ought to be quiet under

3

God's correcting hand, he may, without violating contentment, complain to God. As an ancient writer put it, "Though not with a tumultuous clamor and shrieking out in a confused passion, yet in a quiet, still, submissive way he may open his heart to God." Likewise he may explain his sad condition to his Christian friends, telling them how God has dealt with him and what a burden the hardship is, so they may console him.

*Contentment is not opposed to looking for help or otherwise using practical methods to overcome one's misfortunes, as long as the methods are lawful.* I may try to escape by using godly methods, while waiting on the Lord to reveal whether it will be his will to change my situation. Certainly, looking for help with submission and holy resignation of spirit is not opposed to the quietness which God requires in a contented spirit. This means we seek to be delivered when, and as, and how God wills, so that our wills are melted into his.

But what is this quietness of spirit opposed to?

*Contentment is opposed to grumbling and fretting about what God brings us,* as the discontented Israelites did. If we cannot bear such behavior in our children or employees, much less can God bear it in us.

*Contentment is opposed to being vexed and upset to a degree beyond grumbling.* A heathen said, "A wise man may grieve for, but not be vexed with his afflictions." There is a vast difference between a kindly grieving and being stirred up with vexation.

*Contentment is opposed to agitation of spirit,* when the thoughts are distracted and work in a confused manner. Then the emotions are like the unruly crowd in the book of Acts, who did not know for what purpose they had come together. The Lord expects you to be silent under his discipline, and as it says in Acts 19:36, "You ought to keep calm and to do nothing rash."

*Contentment is opposed to an unsettled and unstable spirit* that distracts you from your duty to God, self, and others. We should prize duty more highly than to be distracted by every trivial incident. A Christian values every service to God too much for that. Yes, in the eyes of the world and of natural reason, some services to God may seem to be a waste of time, or beneath one's dignity, or foolish. But the authority of God's command so overawes a Christian that he is willing to spend his strength on his duties.

4

Martin Luther said that ordinary good works done in faith are more precious than heaven and earth. If this is so, then a Christian should not be diverted from such works by little matters that would make him discontent. He should answer every distraction and temptation, as Nehemiah answered Sanballat, Geshem, and Tobiah when they would have hindered the building of Jerusalem's wall: "I am doing a great work and I cannot come down. Why should the work stop while I leave it and come down to you?" (Nehemiah 6:3).

*Contentment is opposed to distracting, heart-consuming cares.* Someone blessed by grace values union with Christ and work for God so much that he will not willingly allow anything to derail them. He wants the Bible message to take such full possession of his soul that he will not allow fear and bad news to get a grip on him and so cause division and struggling within him.

An eminent man will allow petitioners to stand outside his doors, but he will not let them come in and make a noise in his den or bedroom when he has deliberately withdrawn from all worldly business. So someone with a well-tempered spirit may inquire about things outside in the world, allowing them to touch lightly on his thoughts. But on no account will he allow an intrusion into the private room of the soul, which should be wholly reserved for Jesus Christ as his inward temple.

*Contentment is opposed to sinking discouragements.* When things do not turn out according to expectation, when events are so discouraging that we see little to hope for, then a man begins to reason like the doubting man in II Kings 7:2: "If the Lord should make windows in heaven, could this thing be?" We never consider that God can open the eyes of the blind with clay and spittle, that he can work above, beyond, and even contrary to the natural order of things. He often makes our attempts wither like flowers, and in their place brings about improbable things, so that the glory may be all his. If his people need miracles to save them, God provides them as easily as he does their daily bread.

The source of God's blessing is often a secret from us, so that we do not know which direction it will come from. Consider the scripture: "You shall not see wind nor shall you see rain; yet that valley shall be filled with water..." (II Kings 3:17). God wants us to

5

depend on him though we cannot imagine how relief may come; otherwise, we do not show a quiet spirit. When you are troubled, do not let your heart sink under it. To the extent that your heart sinks and you are discouraged because of some trouble, just that much you need to learn this lesson of contentment.

*Contentment is opposed to sinful shiftiness and shirking to get relief and help.* Examples of this include King Saul sneaking off to see the witch of Endor for a séance (I Samuel 28:6-8), and also when he offered sacrifice too early, before Samuel came to legitimize it (I Samuel 13:7-14). Good King Jehoshaphat made alliance with the unrighteous King Ahaziah (II Chronicles 20:35). King Asa went to Benhadad, King of Syria, for help, not relying on the Lord (II Chronicles 16:7,8), though previously God had delivered a million man Ethiopian army into Asa's hands (II Chronicles 14:12). The patriarch Jacob joined with his mother in lying to Isaac (Genesis 27). Not content to wait for God's time and use God's methods, he hurried matters by using trickery to grab the blessing which God intended for him.

Because of corruption within us and the weakness of our faith, many of us behave this way. We refuse to always trust God and follow him in everything. This is why the Lord often brings Christians pains and sorrows, as in the case of Jacob, though in the end they receive mercy.

Your worldly thought may be, "I don't care how I'm saved, just so I'm freed from this misfortune." Is that not often the case, when any trouble or hardship comes? Do you not think like this? "Oh, if I could only be saved from this misfortune somehow, I would not care how!" You are far from being quiet. This sinful shiftiness is opposed to the quietness which God requires in a contented person.

*Finally, contentment is opposed to rebellion of the heart against God.* That is the most abominable course you can take. I hope many of you have learned enough of contentment to restrain you from such an extreme. Yet the truth is that not only the wicked but sometimes even Christians descend to this when some hardship lasts a long time and is very severe, hitting them, so to speak, where they live. They feel an uprising against God in their hearts, their thoughts begin to bubble, and their emotions begin to rise in rebellion.

6

This is especially the case with those who, besides being inwardly corrupt, are easily depressed. The Devil goes to work on both the corruption and the melancholy, and though they may be greatly blessed by grace, yet under hardship they may rebel some against God. Christian quietness is opposed to all these things.

**Contentment is in the *spirit*.**

Contentment is a condition of the spirit controlled by grace. Contentment is a soul business.

*It is a grace that spreads through the whole soul.* It begins in your judgment. That is, your judgment quiets your heart—in your judgment you are satisfied. It is a good beginning to be satisfied in your judgment and understanding so as to be able to say, "This misfortune is the will of God, and it's suitable to my condition and best for me. Although I don't see the reason for it, still I'm satisfied in my judgment about it." Then it progresses to the thoughts. As my judgment is satisfied, so my thoughts are kept in order. And so this good progression continues through the whole soul.

In some people the resulting contentment is only partial. It is not the whole soul but just a part of it that has contentment. Many a man may be satisfied in his judgment about a thing who cannot for the life of him go on to rule his emotions, thoughts, or will. I do not doubt that many of you know this in your own experience if you have kept track of your inner selves. When hardship comes, you say, "I can thank God and I *should be* content. Yes, in my judgment I'm satisfied that my situation is good. But I can't for the life of me rule my thoughts, will, and emotions. My heart's more heavy and sad than it should be, even though my judgment is satisfied."

This seems to be how David felt in Psalm 42: "Why are you in despair, O my soul? And why have you become disturbed within me?" As far as his judgment went he was satisfied about God's care for him, and he saw no way to defend his discontentment. "Hope in God for I shall yet praise him, the help of my countenance and my God." So David had enough to quiet him, and that carried the day with his judgment, but he could get no further. He could not get this grace of contentment to continue through his soul.

Sometimes you have to move heaven and earth just to convince a troubled person to take the first step, to judge his situation worthy of contentment. If you say he has no cause to be so upset, then, "Oh, no cause?" he replies. "Then there is no cause for anyone to be upset. No one has ever suffered as I have!" He has a hundred reasons to run away from what you say to him, so that you cannot so much as get at his judgment to satisfy him.

But there is plenty of hope in achieving contentment if once your judgment is satisfied, if you can sit down and say, "I see good reason to be contented." Yet even when you have gotten so far, you may still have a lot of ground to cover. Our thoughts and emotions are so disruptive that our judgments are not always able to rule them. That is what makes me say that contentment is an inward condition of spirit. The whole soul—judgment, thoughts, will, and emotions—is satisfied and quiet. I suppose that a glance at this subject tells you it is a lesson you need to learn, and that if contentment is like this, then it is not easy to obtain.

*Spiritual contentment comes from the condition of the soul.* One's contentment does not come so much as a result of someone's outward arguments or from any outside help as it does from the attitude of the heart. Bring a disturbed person some wonderful thing to please him, and perhaps it will calm him and he will be contented. It is what you bring that calms him down, not the disposition of his spirit. But when a Christian is content in the right way, it comes from his attitude more than any persuasion or possession in the world.

Compare it to this: Being content because of some external matter is like wearing clothes warmed by the fire. But being content due to an inward attitude of the soul is like the warmth that a man's clothes have from the natural heat of his body. A healthy man gets dressed, and perhaps at first on a cold morning his clothes feel cold. But soon they are warmed by his body heat. But when a sickly man gets dressed, his clothes do not get warm even after a long time. He must warm them by the fire, and even then they will soon be cold again.

So it is with contentment. Some are very grace-filled, and so when misfortune comes, though at first it seems chilling, after a while their attitude makes it easy. They are quiet about it and do not complain of any discontent. Others do not have this good attitude, so misfortune is very cold and troubling to them. Maybe if you try persuasions on

8

them (like the fire that heats the clothes), they will be calm for a while. But sadly, if they lack a grace-filled attitude, the warmth will not last long. When it comes from one's spirit, that is true contentment.

*The condition of spirit determines the lasting character of contentment.* Contentment is not just a passing good mood. You find many who, in a good mood, will be very serene. But it does not last, because it is not the persistent tone of their spirits to be holy when troubles come. The Christian who constantly carries himself serenely has learned this lesson of contentment. Otherwise his Christianity is worth nothing. After all, anyone—even the worst tempered—will be tranquil when in a good mood.

### Contentment is a *grace-filled* condition.

Genuine spiritual contentment is a combination of all graces, of many spiritual blessings from God, such as faith, humility, love, patience, wisdom, and hope. This condition of spirit is in opposition to three things that might be mistaken for it:

*True contentment is in opposition to the natural quietness of many people.* Some are more still and quiet by nature. But watch them and you will see that they are also sluggish to do anything good. But when contentment of heart springs from grace, the heart is very quick and lively to serve God. Such a person is eager to honor God in his heart even in the midst of his troubles.

This also distinguishes real contentment from *a sturdy resolution not to be troubled.* Though you may have such stout character, do you make it a matter of conscience to honor God during your troubles, and is that the source of your resolution? The desire and care you have to honor God during misfortune is what calms the soul, and this is what others lack.

*A quietness derived only from reasoning will not serve the purpose either.* It is said of Socrates, though he was only a heathen, that he would never so much as change his expression regardless of what happened. He got this power over his spirit merely by the strength of reason and morality. But grace-filled contentment comes from principles beyond the strength of reason.

9

I will give you just one sign of the difference between natural and spiritual contentment. Though those who are content in a natural way manage to overcome their emotions when hardships come, they are just as content when they commit sin against God. Whether it is their own troubles or God dishonored, it is all the same to them; whether they themselves are crossed or whether God is crossed. But a grace-filled person who is contented with his own hardship will nevertheless rise up in indignation when God is dishonored.

**Contentment comes from submitting *freely*.**

Three points need to be made about this freedom of spirit:
*The heart is readily won over.* When someone does a thing freely, he does not need a lot of persuasion to get him to do it. Many who are experiencing hardship may be brought to a state of contentment with much effort. But when a man is free about something, only mention it and immediately he does it. So he will be content as soon as he comes to see that it is the will of God.

*It is freely, that is, not by constraint.* This is not 'forced patience.' Though some will tell you that you *must* be content because, "This is the will of God and you cannot help it," that is a poor way for Christians to talk. Yet, when Christians come to visit one another, they say, "Friend, you must be content." No, rather it should be, "Readily and freely I'll be content. It suits me to yield to God and be content. I find it's a thing that comes naturally." You should answer your friend like that.

*This freedom is in opposition to mere stupidity.* A person may be contented from lack of sense. But a grace-filled person has sense enough, and yet is contented and therefore free.

**Contentment comes from *submission*.**

What does it mean to submit to God's management of your life? You see your own unruliness, that when God brings you misfortune you choose to react with scowls of discontentment. You then say to yourself, "What, will I be above God? Isn't this God's will, and should my will be regarded as more important than his? O soul, keep under! Keep low! You're under God's feet, and stay under his feet! Keep under God's authority, majesty, sovereignty, and power!"

**Contentment means *taking pleasure* in God's management.**

I feel the hardship, I wish that God might end it in his due time, and I may try practical methods to overcome it myself. In the meantime I am pleased to the extent that God's will is in it. Not only do I see that I should be content with this misfortune, but I see that there is good in it. To acknowledge the justice of it is not enough. You must say, "The Lord's will is good." This does not just apply later after you actually see the good that comes of it, but you should be able to say at the time, "It's good that I'm troubled. Through the mercy of God my condition is good." The height of this art of contentment is to be able to say, "Well, my condition and troubles are what they are, and very serious and painful; yet, through God's mercy, I'm in a good condition, and he's bringing me good regardless."

"Great wealth is in the house of the righteous, but trouble is in the income of the wicked" (Proverbs 15:6). Here is a scripture to show that a grace-filled person may claim he is in a good condition, no matter what that condition may be. The righteous man's house may be a poor hovel, and perhaps he has scarcely a stool to sit on, a bed to lie on, or a dish to eat from. Yet the Holy Ghost says, "Great wealth is in the house of the righteous," even if his house is plundered of everything in it. A righteous man can never be made so poor, cannot have his house so rifled and despoiled, but lots of treasure will remain within. He has the presence and the blessing of God, and that is ample treasure. He is better off than the wealthiest man in the world who has rich tapestries, finely crafted furniture, cupboards full of silver plate, and so forth.

Take the example of Paul who, poor man, at times did not have clothing or bread, and who was put in the stocks, whipped, and cruelly used. Yet he wrote of himself as "poor yet making many rich, as having nothing yet possessing all things" (II Corinthians 6:10). A Christian has reason to be pleased with whatever God brings him. He says, "The Lord knows how to arrange things better than I do. He sees further than I do. I only see the present, but the Lord sees into the far

11

future. And how do I know but that, if not for this misfortune, I would have been lost? I know that God's love suits a time of troubles just as well as it does prosperity." A contented person reasons in this way.

**Contentment is submitting to *God's* management.**

In everything the contented person looks up to God. He does not look earthward at secondary causes of things, to say that some person did it, that it was the unreasonableness of so and so or barbaric treatment by someone or other. He looks up to God. Submitting to God's management, he sees his wisdom in everything.

**Finally, true contentment is in *every situation*.**

*Submitting to God in whatever kind of hardship comes to us.* Suppose I were to go to everyone in my congregation and ask, "Would you submit to God's management of your life in any condition he would choose for you?" Every one of them would say, "God forbid that I wouldn't!" But there is a great deal of deceit in bland assurances. In general you would submit to anything, but what if it happens to be that particular case that pains you the most? Then, "Anything but that!" But true contentment holds on even through whatever pains you the most.

It may be that the trouble God brings is caused by your child. "Oh, if it had only been my possessions instead!" you say. Or, "I would rather it had been my health." But if it *is* your health, "Oh, if it had been in my business, I would not have cared!" But you cannot carve your own serving. We must be content with whatever particular troubles God brings us.

*Submitting to God as to the timing and length of the misfortune.* "Maybe I could submit and be content," someone says, "except that this hardship has lasted such a long time that my patience is worn out and broken." Perhaps this long-lasting trouble is spiritual, and you say, "If this had been just for a short time, I could submit; but to seek God's face in prayer for so long and he still doesn't respond, oh how will I bear it?" But we should not be our own managers for the timing of deliverance from troubles any more than for the kind of deliverance or the source.

12

In Ezekiel 1:28 the prophet says, "And when I saw it, I fell on my face and heard a voice speaking." The prophet was on his face before God, but how long must he lie there? "Then He said to me, 'Son of man, stand on your feet that I may speak with you!' As He spoke to me the Spirit entered me and set me on my feet" (Ezekiel 2:1-2). Ezekiel had to lie there until God gave him permission to stand, and what is more, until God's Spirit entered him and enabled him to stand. So when God casts us down, we too must be content to lie there till he gives us permission and the strength of his Spirit to stand.

Noah experienced troubles on the Ark, being shut up there with all kinds of animals for a year. When the flood waters subsided, he still was not allowed to leave the Ark until God said so. We too, when shut up in hardships, must wait for God to open the door. We should be willing to stay, because God has put us in, and he will bring us out.

In Joshua 4:10 we read that the priests that carried the Ark of the Covenant stood in the midst of the Jordan's dry riverbed, no doubt fearing that the waters of the river, held back by God's miracle, would be released on them. The rest of the people were allowed to hastily pass over to safety on the far bank, and only then were the priests with the ark allowed to pass over. Similarly, because of the present war God has arranged that ministers, judges, and those in public office must stay in danger longer than other people. That ought to make people in a lower position satisfied with what God has assigned them.

*Submitting to God regarding the variety of our condition.* God may give us various misfortunes one after another. We have seen lately that many have had their goods plundered and afterward have fallen sick and died. They had to flee for their lives, and then caught the plague, and if not that then something else. Solitary misfortunes are rare, but they tend to come one right after another. God may strike a man in his possessions, then in his body, then in his reputation, wife, child, or dear friend. When there is such a variety of troubles, one's condition changes tremendously, up and down, this way and that, and such is the truest test of a Christian. It was said of Cato, a heathen, that no one ever saw him disturbed, though he lived in a time when the Roman commonwealth was in turmoil. Oh, that the same could be said of many Christians!

13

I hope that the reader will now say, "Lord, there is more to Christian contentment than I thought, and I have been far from learning this lesson. I've only just learned my ABC's of contentment. I'm only in first grade in Christ's school if I'm enrolled at all." My aim is to show what a great secret there is to Christian contentment and how many lessons there are to be learned, so that we may come to have this heavenly disposition that St. Paul had.

## Chapter 2 - The Secret of Contentment

Some will say, "What you describe is all very well if anyone could achieve it! But is it possible?" Yes, it is possible if you acquire skill in the art of it; and it will not be all that difficult if you understand the secret of it. People do many things in their professions that look very difficult if not impossible, but that is because we do not know the art of it: some twist of the hand that makes it easy. The business of this book is to reveal to you the art and secret of contentment.

Chapter 1 showed that part of our lesson is to learn to make a mixture of joy and sorrow. That is, grace teaches us how to respond to a misfortune in such a way that we feel it and yet have contentment under it.

Aspects of the secret of contentment follow.

### Satisfied, yet unsatisfied

Someone contented in a Christian way is the most contented person in the world, and yet the most dissatisfied in the world. You will ask how that can be. He is the most contented with any lowly condition, and yet he cannot be satisfied with the enjoyment of the whole world. He is content with bread and water, but if God were to give him all the world to rule, he would not be satisfied with that.

Men of the world pursue wealth and think that, if they only had a certain income, they would be content. "If I only had £50,000 a year or £60,000 a year," one says, "I would be satisfied." But a godly man says that, if he had a billion pounds a year, it would not satisfy him.

Yet he can sing and be merry when he has only a crust of bread and a little water. How mysterious godliness is!

When Martin Luther was sent costly gifts by dukes and princes, he refused them, saying, "I did vehemently protest that God should not put me off so; 'tis not that which will content me."

The answer to this puzzle is that a person made for God can be satisfied by nothing else but God. As it says in Philippians 4, verses 7 and 9, "And the peace of God, which surpasses all comprehension, will guard your hearts and minds in Christ Jesus. The things you have learned and received and heard and seen in me, practice these things, and the God of peace will be with you." A worldly man may be satisfied with mere outward peace, though it is not the peace of God. Peace in his country and his business matters would satisfy him. But the godly man says, "Outward peace isn't enough; I must have the peace of God and the God of peace. I must enjoy God, finding in him the source and fountain of my peace. And it's the same with health, life, riches, and safety. Having them isn't enough: I must have the God who provides them." Psalm 73:25 says, "Whom have I in heaven but You? And besides You, I desire nothing on earth." If God gave you not just earth but to rule over the galaxy, it would not be enough to satisfy you unless you had God himself.

**A Christian arrives at contentment not so much by addition as by subtraction.**

He arrives at contentment not by adding to what he has but by subtracting from his desires, so as to make his desires and his circumstances even and equal. A worldly man knows no way to be contented but this: "I have such and such possessions, and if I have this and that added to them, then I'll be content." If he has lost his possessions, he says, "If someone would just give me enough to make up my loss, then I'd be content." But contentment does not come by adding to what you have. For a Christian it is the same whether he gets enough to equal his desires, on the one hand, or whether he lowers his desires to what he already has, on the other. His standing is much the same, for it is just as workable to lower his desires to his circumstances as it is to raise his circumstances to his desires. If a man can bring his wants down as low as his circumstances, to make

16

them even, this is the way of contentment. That is why many godly men who are in lowly circumstances live more sweet and comfortable lives than those who are richer.

Contentment is not always clothed in silk and velvet but sometimes in cotton. Many who once had great estates and lost them have been more content in reduced circumstances than they were before. All that is necessary for this is that a man's spirit be in proportion to his level of income. But no matter how rich God makes you, if he abandons you to the pride of your heart, you will never be contented, for your greed will never allow your spirit and your wealth to rest equal. On the other hand, no matter how poor you may be, if you let God adjust your heart to it, you will be content. Compare it to this: no matter the length of your legs, you will walk smoothly as long as they are of equal length. To have riches and a proud heart, however, is the equivalent of one short leg and one long!

Even the heathen philosophers of antiquity could say that the best wealth comes through restraint of desires. So this is the art of contentment: not to try to add to our circumstances, but to subtract from our desires. You are rich if you know that your present circumstances are the best, being content by way of subtraction and not addition.

**A Christian becomes content not by getting rid of his burden but by adding another burden to it.**

You think there is no way to be content but to be rid of your burden. "O, if only this burden were gone! O, it's a heavy load, and few know what a burden I have!" But the way of contentment is to add another burden, that is, to burden your heart with your sin. The heavier the load of your sin is, the lighter will be the burden of your hardship, and so you will become content.

Do you call that strange? You think there is no other way to battle your hardship than to make yourself be cheerful and merry and to socialize. But you are deceived; your burden will return. If you want a lightened burden, get alone and examine your heart for sin, and reproach yourself for it. If your burden is because of your possessions, then reproach yourself for the past misuse of what you owned. If it is for your poor health, then reproach yourself for the neglect of your body. And if for any blessings that the Lord has taken away from you, then blame yourself for not having honored God with those blessings when you had them but of having lived shamelessly and carelessly. If you mourn for your sin before the Lord, you will quickly find the burden of your hardship to be lighter than before. Just try it!

Often in a family, when any misfortune comes along, how the sparks fly between husband and wife! It may be due to loss of possessions, bad news from overseas, the ruin of a business partner, or whatever. Or perhaps the spouses are fighting about their children or employees, and there is nothing but quarreling and discontent between them. They feel the burden of their discontent and wish to find a way to live comfortably together. Here is a method I think you have not tried. Get alone and say to one another, "Come, let's humble our souls before God for our sin. We've abused the blessings God gave us, and so he took them away. We've provoked him against us. Let's reproach ourselves for our sin and be humbled before him together." If you were to try that, you would find that the cloud would pass away, the sun would shine upon you, and you would have more contentment than ever before.

If a man's estate is lost, either to plunderers or any other way, how shall he have contentment? By the breaking of his heart. Let his heart be as broken as his estate, for a broken estate and a whole heart (a hard heart) do not go together. But a broken estate and a broken heart suit one another so well that he will be deeply content.

> **It is not so much getting rid of the hardship as transforming it into something else.**

I am referring to making use of the hardship, though it remains. To a worldly person the only way to contentment is by removing the hardship.

"O, if only it were gone!"

"No," replies a grace-filled person, "God has taught me how to be content though the trouble continues."

Grace has the power to turn this trouble into good, to take away the sting and the poison of it. Suppose your possessions are lost: Well, is there no way to be contented until your possessions are restored and

18

your poverty removed? Yes, certainly, Christianity teaches contentment though poverty continues. It will teach you how to turn your poverty to spiritual riches. You will still be poor in outward possessions, but this will be altered so that, though before it was a natural evil to you, it becomes a spiritual benefit. And so you come to be content.

St. Ambrose said, "Even poverty is riches to holy men." Godly men get more riches out of their poverty than they ever got out of their revenues. Out of all their trading in this world they never had such incomes as they have had out of their poverty. So you do not find a single godly man who came out of misfortune worse than when he went into it; though for a while he was shaken, yet at last he was the better for it.

But a great many godly men have been worse for their prosperity! Almost every godly man you read of in scripture was worse for having wealth. (The exceptions are Daniel and Nehemiah.) So you see it is no strange thing for someone who is grace-filled to benefit from misfortune.

Martin Luther has a similar observation in his commentary on Galatians 5:17. He says that a Christian "becomes a mighty worker and a wonderful creator, that is, to create out of heaviness joy, out of terror comfort, out of sin righteousness, and out of death life." He brings light out of darkness. At the Creation it was God's prerogative to exercise the creative power to command the light to shine out of darkness. Because his grace toward Christians is part of his divine nature, it carries an impression of that divinity that he imparts to us. In this way we share in God's ability to turn darkness into light, that is, to bring good out of evil (and so become content). God has given a Christian such power that he can turn hardships into blessings, can turn the water of misfortune into the wine of heavenly consolation.

If you look at this in a worldly way, you have to call it ridiculous. So when we say of grace that it can turn poverty into riches, making poverty a gainful employment, a worldly person replies, "You can keep that job for yourself!" But be careful not to speak scornfully of the ways of God; grace *does* have the power to turn hardships into blessings. Of two men with the same trouble, to one it will be like gall and wormwood, yet to the other it will be wine and honey;

19

delightfulness, joy, advantage, and riches. This is the secret of attaining contentment, not so much by removing the evil as by transforming it into good.

**A Christian achieves contentment not by making up his shortages but by doing whatever work his situation calls for.**

I lack many things. I want this and that comfort. Well, how shall I come to be satisfied and content? A worldly person thinks, "I must have what I lack or it's impossible for me to be content." But a grace-filled person says, "What is my responsibility in the situation God has put me into? Not long ago I was in prosperous circumstances, but God changed that. Now what am I to *do*? What now are my duties? Let me strive to perform those duties with the resources available. Others fixate on what disturbs and disquiets them, and so they grow more and more discontented; but let me think of what my responsibility is."

A man who has lost his wealth says, "If I just had my money back, how I'd use it for God's glory! He has made me see that I didn't honor him with my possessions as much I should have. If I just had my wealth back, I'd do better than I did before." But this may be no more than a tempting fantasy. You should think instead: "What does God require of me in my present circumstances?" You should labor to become content by working on achievable tasks. I know of nothing more effective for gaining contentment.

Those who think they will gain contentment by daydreaming about other circumstances are like children who climb a hill to try to touch the clouds. So it is with many who think, "If I were in such and such circumstances, then I'd be happy." Maybe they get into those very circumstances and yet are as far from contentment as ever. So then they think of yet other circumstances to make them happy, arrive at that situation, and are still unhappy. No, no, let me be content to say, "Though I'm in a low position, I'll serve God where I am. God brought me into this situation, and I want to serve him in it."

Acts 13:36 says, "For David, after he had served the purpose of God in his own generation, fell asleep." We should do likewise, and that means serving from the position God has placed us in, no matter what that may be. So like David I shall aim to live and die peaceably and comfortably, by being careful to serve God.

**A grace-filled person is contented when his will and desires melt into God's.**

In this sense, he has his desires satisfied although he does not obtain what he desired before. He becomes satisfied because he makes his will match God's. This is rather more than submitting to the will of God. When you can, so to speak, deed your will over to God, you will necessarily be contented. Others want what they desire, but a grace-filled person will say, "What God wants, I want too. I don't just yield to it, but it's really what I want."

Suppose a man were to transfer his debt over to someone else. If the person assuming the debt for him is satisfied, then of course he is too. It is the same between a Christian and God as regards transfer of the Christian's will. The Christian makes his will over to God, and if God is satisfied, then the Christian is. He no longer has a will of his own; it is melted into God's will. What a sweet satisfaction that brings!

You will say, "That's too hard!" But let me further explain. This works because the good that relates to my life, comforts, happiness, glory, and riches is actually more God's good than it is mine. One can say, "If God has glory, I have glory; if he has riches then I'm rich; if he is magnified, so am I; if he is satisfied, I'm satisfied; his wisdom and holiness are mine; and therefore his will must be mine and mine his."

"He chooses our inheritance for us" (Psalm 47:4).

**The secret of contentment is not in bringing something from outside to make me more comfortable, but in purging out something within.**

Worldly people must have something from outside to content them. But a godly man says, "Let me expel something that is in me, and then I'll be contented." This is like a medicine that causes someone to purge. The way to contentment is to purge out your lusts and bitterness. The Apostle James says, "What is the source of quarrels and conflicts among you? Is not the source your pleasures that wage

21

war in your members?" (James 4:1). It is not so much things outside as what is inside. Not all the storms in the atmosphere can cause an earthquake, but it results from underground pressures. Similarly, if the lusts within your heart were expelled, you would be contented.

**A grace-filled heart lives on the dew of God's blessing.**

A Christian can get food that the world does not know about; he is fed secretly by the dew of the blessing of God. In this way a poor man is more contented than his rich neighbor.

Here are five ways a man finds contentment in what he has, although he may have very little:

*The love of God accompanies what the man has.* Suppose a king were to send a quarter of beef from his own table as a gift to one of his courtiers. Because it is a token of the king's favor, the courtier would be more pleased with this one gift than with a large and steady supply of foodstuffs. If a woman's husband is at sea and sends her some token of his love, to her it is worth far more than all she has in her house. Similarly, God's people enjoy every good thing they have as a token of his love, and so it is very sweet to them.

Non-Christians have what they enjoy as God's common providence. They have what they have and no more: meat, drink, houses, clothes, money, and that is all. But a godly person has an extra, sanctified use of what God gives him. God himself accompanies what he has and draws his heart nearer to him. Along with the worldly things he enjoys comes the secret dew of God's love and holiness.

*A godly person gets what he has for free.* A godly man is like an innkeeper's child who gets his housing, food, and other necessities for free, while inn guests have to pay for everything. It may be that the child's food is not as rich and delicious as the guests' is. Yet, though the guests may have fine food—boiled, roasted, and baked—they have to pay for it all. There will be a reckoning! In the same way, God's people may have poor food, but God their father provides it for free, in the sense that they are accounted debtless concerning it when they die. In contrast, the wicked in all their pomp, pride, and finery have what they ask for at God's inn, but there must come a reckoning for everything. They must pay for it all before they leave. Is it not better to have a little free of cost, than to have to pay for everything?

*A godly man has what he has by the purchase of Jesus Christ.* He has a right to it in a way that a wicked man does not. Wicked men also have a right to what they have, but it is a mere donation: God gives it to them. In contrast, the right that the saints have is a right by purchase. It is paid for, and it is their own, and they may in a holy way claim whatever they need. Compare it to this: a criminal condemned to die is granted a last meal. Though he has no right to a crumb of it, yet he is not stealing his supper. So it is with the wicked: they have forfeited their rights to the comforts of the world, they are condemned by God as criminals, and are going to execution. But if God gives them anything to keep them alive, they cannot be said to be thieves. The child of God, on the other hand, eats of what is his own, because it is purchased by Christ. Before you buy your food at the market, Christ has bought it from God the Father with his blood.

*The little that a Christian may have is just a first installment*, guaranteeing that the rest will follow, of all the glory that is reserved for him. If a man has just a pound given to him as the first installment of a vast fortune, is that not better than if he had a thousand pounds and nothing to follow? So every comfort that the saints have in this world is a first installment to them of the eternal blessings that the Lord has in store for them.

Just as every trouble that the wicked have in this world is only the beginning of eternal sorrows that they are likely to have in hell, so every comfort you have is a forerunner of the eternal blessings you will have with God in heaven. The present sweetness of God's Spirit to you is a sample of eternal comforts. Your happiness at home with spouse, children, and friends is a forerunner of eternal life. If this is so, no wonder a Christian is contented; but this is a mystery to the wicked.

By all this you may see the meaning of Proverbs 16:8, "Better is a little with righteousness than great income with injustice."

**A Christian has the dew of God's blessing in more than just good things.**

Even in the evils that come to a Christian, he can see love. He can enjoy the sweetness of love in his misfortunes as well as in his blessings. The truth is that the hardships of God's people come from the same eternal love that sends them blessings. St. Jerome said, "He is a happy man who is beaten when the stroke is a stroke of love." All God's strokes are strokes of love and mercy. "All the paths of the Lord are lovingkindness and truth to those who keep His covenant and His testimonies" (Psalm 25:10). Grace enables a man to understand the counsel of God and so to see the love of God in every misfortune as well as in prosperity. This is a mystery to worldly people. They see no such thing. They think God loves them when he prospers them and makes them rich, but they think he does not love them when he distresses them. Grace enables men to see love even in God's frown, and so they gain contentment.

**A godly man has contentment as a spiritual mystery.**

This is because he sees his troubles come from the same love that sent him Jesus Christ, and so they are sanctified in Jesus. He sees all the sting and venom taken out of them by the virtue of Christ, the mediator between God and man.

He reasons like this: "What is my problem? Is it poverty? Jesus did not have a house to live in. My poverty is sanctified by his. By faith I see the curse, sting, and venom taken out of my poverty because of the poverty of Jesus Christ. Or am I disgraced or dishonored? Is my good name taken away? Yet Jesus himself was called Beelzebub and a Samaritan, and they said he had a devil in him. Every foul slander was cast on him, and this was for my benefit, so that I might have the disgrace that is cast on me as something sanctified to me."

Another sort of person is overwhelmed by dishonor and disgrace. When others slander him, he has no other way to ease himself than to abuse them back. But a Christian reflects that, though others verbally abuse him, they also abused Jesus. "And what am I in comparison to Christ? And the curse of it was taken from me through Christ's subjection to that evil."

"Am I in great bodily pain?" he asks himself. "Jesus had as great pain in his body." Suppose you lie there vexing and fretting yourself and cannot bear the pain. Well, are you a Christian? Have you ever tried to apply your faith by considering all the pains and sufferings that Jesus suffered? That is how a Christian gets contentment when in pain. Have you ever been astonished to see someone bear with severe pains cheerfully? Well, this is how it is done.

Or if you are afraid of death, the way to contentment is to apply your faith to Jesus' death. Or it may be that you have a troubled soul and God withdraws from you; still you must apply your faith to the sufferings Jesus endured in his soul. Remember that he sweat drops of water and blood, that he was in agony in his spirit, and that he found that even God the Father was about to forsake him.

To place your faith in Jesus brings contentment, and is that not a mystery to worldly people? A person blessed by God finds that contentment comes from a source that is a spiritual mystery.

## A Yet Deeper Mystery

A godly person gets contentment by drawing strength from Jesus; he bears his burden by drawing strength from someone else! Now this is quite a riddle. Philosophers would call it ridiculous to say that, if you are under a burden, you must draw strength from someone else. They could understand having someone bear the burden for you, but that someone else's might could strengthen you they would think absurd. But by faith in Jesus a Christian draws Jesus' strength into his own soul and is therefore able to bear any burden. Jesus expects us to do this, to draw on him for virtue and strength. If the burden is doubled, the Christian's strength can be *tripled*, so that it will feel lighter to him, not heavier.

When we are crushed by troubles we cry, "Oh, I can't bear it!" Though this is true of your own strength, how do you know what you might do with the strength of Jesus? Yes, you cannot bear it, but do you think that Christ could not bear it? You say, "But can I really have the strength of Jesus?" Yes, due to your faith. The scripture says that the Lord is our strength (Psalm 28:7). In fact the Bible has many verses that say that. In Colossians 1:11, Paul prayed for the saints that

25

they might be "strengthened with all power, according to His glorious might, for the attaining of all steadfastness and patience." So do not try to get by on the strength of your puny mind and body. Be strengthened with all might.

**A godly person enjoys God in everything he has, and he knows how to make up all he lacks in God.**

In whatever a Christian has he has God too, but there is more to it than that. What if the little a man has is taken from him? People say, "Nothing comes from nothing," but if God's children have everything taken from them, they can make up all they lack in God himself. Some poor man is the victim of plunderers who carry off everything he owns. What shall he do now that all is gone? But when all is gone, there is an art and skill that godliness teaches, to make up all losses in God.

Many whose houses have been burned go around gathering donations, and so from many people get a little, but a godly man knows where to go to restore all, that is, in God. In this way he may enjoy the essence of the same good and comfort he had before, for a godly man does not live so much in himself as he lives in God. If cut off from the stream, he goes to the fountain and makes it all up there. God is his all in all. The Lord says to you, "Your estate is plundered and you feel the lack. But aren't I as good as ten homes to you? I am in place of all to you, and more than that, you have it all again in me."

Created things were really never more to you than a conduit, a pipe that conveyed God's goodness to you. God says, "If the pipe is broken, come to me, the fountain, and drink." Though sunbeams are taken away, the sun remains the same in the sky as it ever was.

God is satisfied in the fullness that is himself. Since he is your portion (Lamentations 3:24), you too may be contented with him alone. And this may be the reason your outward comforts are taken from you, so that God may become all in all to you. Maybe those comforts competed with God for your affection, so that a great part of the stream of your affection ran toward them. God wants the full stream to run to him now

When a man has a weak stream of water coming to a faucet, he will shut off the other pipes of his house so the flow will come strongly to

26

where he wants it. Perhaps, then, God has shut off your other pipes so that your heart might flow only to him. Or suppose your children's nanny is stealing away their hearts, perhaps by feeding them treats and giving them presents. If you send her away, soon their affections will run again to their own mother. So God turns our affections away from created things and toward himself.

The happiness of those who are in heaven is to have God be all in all. They do not have houses, lands, money, meat, drink, or clothes. They do not need them because God is all in all to them immediately. Now while you live in this world, you may come to enjoy much of the same life that is in heaven, and what is that but the enjoyment of God as all in all? As it says in Revelation 21:22: "I saw no temple in it, for the Lord God the Almighty and the Lamb are its temple. And the city has no need of the sun or of the moon to shine on it, for the glory of God has illumined it, and its lamp is the Lamb."

That verse speaks of a glorious condition that the Church is likely to experience here in this world; that is, it does not speak of heaven, but of a glorious status here. The proof is that it says immediately after this that the kings of the earth will bring their glory and honor into the city, which they could not do to heaven; therefore this passage must refer to this world. There will be such a time here in this world when God shall be all in all, and there will be comparatively little need of created things such as we experience now. So Christians now should try to live that life as nearly as possible, that is, to make up all losses in God.

Please consider this mystery, so it will be real to your heart during such troubled times as these. You would find this privilege provided by grace to be worth thousands of worlds. In Genesis 33 Jacob and Esau both say that they have enough possessions for them, but the Hebrew word Jacob uses is different. Jacob's word signifies having *all* things, and yet Jacob was poorer than Esau! It would be a shame for a Christian to say less than Jacob did. Let him say, "I don't just have enough, but I have all." This corresponds with the saying: He has all things who has him who has all things.

Another way of looking at this is to say that a godly man has all-sufficiency within himself. Not from himself but in himself. This is so because he has so much of God within him that there is enough to make up for all his outward wants. Though he lacks music, he has a songbird in his soul that makes melody enough. He has the Kingdom of God within him (Luke 17:21). He may be widely slandered, but within him he has that which makes up for the lack of a good name and is better than a thousand witnesses on his behalf.

**A godly man gets contentment from the Biblical covenant that God has made with him.**

There is no condition godly people can be in, but there is some promise or other in the scripture to help them. Go to those promises and get your supply from them. Plead the promises God has made. From among the many Bible verses applicable I choose just one, Psalm 91:10, about the plague. Those with the plague are in quarantine; they cannot have the comfort of visits from friends. But we read, "No evil will befall you, nor will any plague come near your tent." And in verses five and six it states that you will not be afraid of the pestilence. Though you may say this is a promise of protection from plague, notice that two things are combined: protection from evil and from the plague. The sum of it is that the *evil* of plague shall not come near you.

Yes, you will say that the plague does come to many godly people, and how can they make any use of this scripture? Instead this is a scripture to trouble them with, since the plague comes as near them as anyone else. To a Christian stricken with the plague I offer these answers:

*The promises of outward deliverance that were made to God's people during Old Testament times were to be understood then much more literally.* They were fulfilled more literally than now in the time of the gospel when God makes up their value with equivalent mercy. Though the ancient Israelites had, as we do, a covenant of grace and eternal life in Christ, yet I think they had this other covenant too, one for outward things. By this Old Testament covenant, God dealt with them according to their actions, either by giving them outward prosperity or outward hardships, more so than now, in a more immediate and set way.

*Perhaps someone's faith is not enough for this promise of deliverance to apply to him.* Such lack of faith may result in hardships

28

even in this Christian era of the New Testament promises. Thus, for example, Zacharias was stricken with muteness because he did not believe (Luke 1:20). You will say that no one should presume to claim deliverance from worldly hardships because of his faith, and that is certainly so. Nevertheless, a Christian may plead for deliverance, believing that regardless of the outcome, God will make it good in his own way. Perhaps you have not even tried to hope through faith, and so because of that, this promise is not fulfilled to you.

When God makes such a promise it comes with three reservations. First, that regardless of the promise, he has liberty to make use of anything for your discipline. Second, that he has liberty to make use of your wealth, freedom, or even your lives for his own ends. Third, he has liberty to use your possessions in such a way as to show that his ways are unsearchable and his judgments past finding out. God reserves these three things in his hand.

You ask what good it is, then, to have such a promise? The answer is that, though the misfortune may come to you, yet the evil of it shall be taken away from you. If God makes use of your misfortune to  achieve his other purposes, still he does it so as to make it up to you in some other way. Compare it to this. Suppose you have given your child something, but afterwards you find you have a use for it, and you tell him to give it back to you.

"Why, father?" your child may say. "You gave it to me."

"But I must have it," you say, "and I'll make it up to you in some other way."

Your child does not think your love is a bit less to him. So when God promises you his protection, and something bad happens anyway, it is only as if he said, "Yes, I gave you that, but let me have it and I'll make it up to you in some other way that will be just as good." He says, "Let me have your health, liberty, and life, and I'll make it up to you."

Another consideration is this. Whenever the plague or pestilence comes to those who have such a promise of protection, it is because God has some special purpose he is accomplishing. He requires them to search and examine to find out the meaning of it. And so much can be learned from such searching that his people may calm their hearts even in this illness. God has a use for your life and intends to bring

29

out his glory in some way that you do not understand. Since he comes in a fatherly way of discipline, you will be satisfied. Thus a Christian who consults the Bible satisfies his soul even under such a heavy burden from God.

Worldly people do not think the Bible's power and healing virtue apply to their worrisome cares and troubled spirits. Godly people find it to be a salve for all their wounds.

Another aspect of contentment through the covenant with God is this. A Christian may make up what he lacks in creature comforts from what he finds in himself. If he lacks good cheer and feasting, he has the peace of his conscience as a continual feast. If he lacks melody, a songbird within him provides the most lyrical and delightful music. Or does he lack honor? His good conscience is equal to a thousand witnesses to his integrity. Regardless of what he lacks, he has a Kingdom in himself, enough to make anyone's heart content.

When you want to comfort your Christian friends in their troubles, you tell them, "You have heaven to look forward to." But even at present a heaven is in the souls of Christians. No soul goes to heaven unless heaven has come to it first. In contrast, those who depend completely on things of this world for contentment are in a miserable condition. You know that rich men are serenely happy if they do not need to go out and buy things piecemeal. Their estates are already stocked with everything needed or desired: mutton, beef, corn, clothing, and everything else. That is their happiness. But a Christian's happiness is that he has in himself that which can satisfy him more than all these. "And let endurance have its perfect result, so that you may be perfect and complete, lacking in nothing" (James 1:4).

Such a person is like a man who enjoys all the creature comforts at home. God gives him a pleasant house, a good wife, fine walks and gardens, and everything else at home he could desire. So he does not care much for going out. Other men want to go see their friends because they have quarreled at home. The reason many husbands step out is that their wives moan, complaining of all their faults and shortcomings. But we call a man happy who has everything at home as he wants it.

Another comparison is this, that those who live in cramped quarters that are unpleasant and malodorous delight in getting out into fresh air.

Not so if your home is pleasant. This compares to a worldly man who cannot find contentment in his own unpleasant and troubled spirit.

Augustine likens a bad conscience to a scolding wife. A man with a bad conscience does not want to follow its promptings and look into his own soul, but he loves to be out and about, attending to other things. He never looks into himself.

Or compare it to a vase full of water. If you strike it, it will make just a slight noise. But if it is empty it makes a loud noise. So it is with the heart. A heart full of grace and goodness will take stroke after stroke and make no noise, but strike an empty heart and it will make a noise. When some men and women complain so much, always whining, it betrays the emptiness in their hearts.

A man whose bones are filled with marrow, and his veins with good blood, does not complain much in cold weather. So someone with the Spirit of God in his heart has within him what makes him find contentment. Seneca said, "Those things that I suffer will be incredibly heavy when I cannot bear myself." But if I am no burden to myself, if all is quiet in my heart, then I can bear anything. Many, because of their wickedness, have outward burdens, but their greatest burden is the evil of their own hearts. They are not burdened with their sins in a godly way, for that would give them a means to ease their burden. No, they still bear their wickedness in its full power, and so they are burdens to themselves.

Many think, "O if I had what another man has, how happily and comfortably I would live!" But if you are a Christian, whatever your situation, you have enough in yourself.

Some people have achieved financial independence and do not need anyone's help. Many young people work hard to gain such independence and love the idea of living with such freedom. Now a Christian, although he does not enjoy the comforts of this world, may live independently on what he has of God within himself.

Let us continue on the subject of finding contentment through the covenant that God has made with Christians through Christ. Two points need to be made here, and the first is that the Christian gets contentment from the Covenant in general. (The second point will pertain to the *particular* promises in the covenant.)

Concerning the Covenant in general, then, here is a striking scripture. "Truly is not my house so with God? For He has made an everlasting covenant with me, ordered in all things and secured; for all my salvation and all my desire, will He not indeed make it grow?" (II Samuel 23:5). Though not everything in King David's house was as he had wished, he calmed his spirit in the knowledge that God had made an everlasting covenant with him. Are you able to say the same? Even if the plague were to enter your house, could you find comfort in this, that the Lord has made an everlasting covenant with you?

For the things of this world are just momentary, not everlasting. I see a family that was all well just a week ago, and now the plague has swept away many of them, and the rest are left in sadness and mourning. We see that there is no stability in the things of this world, yet the Lord has made with me an everlasting covenant. I find disorder in my heart and in my family; but the everlasting covenant is "ordered in all things" and it is sure.

We can be sure of nothing here in this world, especially in these times. A man certainly cannot feel sure of his wealth. Perhaps some of you have lived well and comfortably before, all was well with you, and you thought your fortress was strong. But within a day or two you see everything taken away from you. What you venture in international trade is risky and needs to be insured. But there is a prestigious insurance office for the godly that charges no fee, except that you use the grace you are given. You may go to this insurance office to cover everything that you risk, either to have the thing itself returned to you, or to be paid for its value.

In the world's insurance offices you cannot be sure to have back the very goods that you insured, but if they are lost, the insurers pledge themselves to make it good to you. This Covenant of grace operates the same. Christians, in all their fears, ought to go to the Covenant to insure their wealth and their lives. You observe that Christians have the same losses that others do, but God pledges to make it all up. And notice what follows: "…for all my salvation." David was saying that what he had by Covenant was his salvation and that he looked on that as enough. He even adds that it is all his desire. He wants nothing else besides this Covenant. Well, surely people must live contentedly who have all their desires? With this Covenant you may not prosper so much in the world as others do, but you can bear that.

It is a special sign of true grace in any man that, when any misfortune comes along, he immediately turns to the Covenant. He does this as naturally as a child who, as soon as it is in danger, does not have to be told to go to his parent.

Now for the *particular* promises in the Covenant of grace. A godly person looks upon every particular promise as coming from the root of the great Covenant of general grace in Christ. Often men concentrate on some particular promises that God will help them when disaster threatens, but they fail to look at the connection of such particular promises to the root, the Covenant of grace. By this they miss a great deal of comfort, for godliness brings promises applicable both to this life and the next. As I wrote of before, we should not rely on the literal performance of promises applying to this life. We know God will make them good some way or other, if not in an outward way then in a spiritual way.

With such considerations in mind, to believe fully and confidently that you are safe from the plague is to lay more weight on the particular promise than it will support. In the New Testament Covenant the promise supports no more than this, that God specially protects his people, that he will deliver them from the evil of such an illness, and that if he does bring plague, it is something extraordinary.

I continue with several particular promises for the contentment of the heart during misfortune.

"When you pass through the waters, I will be with you; and through the rivers, they will not overflow you. When you walk through the fire, you will not be scorched, nor will the flame burn you" (Isaiah 43:2). Though this promise was made in the time of the Old Covenant, it will be made good to Christians now, one way or the other, either literally or in some other way. To demonstrate that it will be made good, I note that this promise in Isaiah is parallel to the promise made to Joshua that God would not fail or forsake him (Joshua 1:5), a promise applied in Hebrews to Christians in the time of the gospel (Hebrews 13:5). Therefore, the promise in Isaiah is also applicable to this time of the gospel.

Regarding Old Testament promises in general, Christians today have an interest in all the promises made to God's people from the beginning of the world. They are our inheritance and pass from one generation to another. Hebrews 13:5 shows plainly that all the promises are our inheritance, that we do not inherit less now than they did in Joshua's time, but more. For Joshua was simply told that God would not leave him or forsake him, but in this verse in Hebrews the original Greek uses five negatives. I will not, not, not, not, not! That is the force of it in the Greek.

In Isaiah 54:17 God promised that no weapon formed against his people would prosper, and that every tongue that shall rise against them in judgment they shall condemn. Notice what follows. "'This is the heritage of the servants of the Lord, and their vindication is from me,' declares the Lord." That is a good promise for a soldier, but we still ought not to put too much weight on the literal sense. Nevertheless, it does say that God's protection is especially over soldiers who are godly. The part about tongues rising against you is about false witnesses. As for the heritage—or inheritance—it may put you in mind of friends who died and never left you a penny, or of your parent who left you no inheritance. Yet you have an inheritance in God's promise. So there is no godly man or woman who is not a great heir.

Therefore, when you look in the Bible and find any promise there, you may consider it your own; just as an heir who rides over many fields and meadows says, "This meadow is my inheritance, and this corn field is my inheritance," and then he sees a fine house and says, "This too." He looks at them with a different eye than some stranger who rides through those fields. A worldly person looks at the scripture promises and dismisses them as mere stories. But every time a godly man reads the Bible and comes to a promise, he ought to lay his finger on it and say, "This is part of my inheritance, it is mine, and I am going to live on it." This ought to make you contented.

**A Christian has contentment by recognizing the glorious things of heaven that are his.**

A Christian has the kingdom of heaven here and now; by his faith the glorious things to come are his in the present. This is how the martyrs had contentment in their sufferings, for some of them said, "Though we've had a hard breakfast, yet we'll have a good dinner: we shall very soon be in heaven." One of them said, "Just shut your eyes

34

and you shall be in heaven at once." And the Apostle Paul said, "Therefore we do not lose heart." Why? Because "momentary light affliction is producing for us an eternal weight of glory far beyond all comparison" (II Corinthians 4:16-17). They see heaven before them and that contents them. Sailors may be badly troubled when out of sight of land, but when they come near shore and see a familiar landmark they are greatly relieved. A godly man in the midst of the waves and storms of his life can see the glory of heaven before him and so contents himself. One drop of the sweetness of heaven is enough to take away all the sourness and bitterness of every trouble in the world.

**Finally, a godly man has contentment by opening his heart to God.**

Others ease their discontent by bad language. Someone crosses them, and they have no way to help themselves but to fire off abuse and bitter words. A godly man, just as aware of his troubles, goes to God in prayer and by opening his heart lets out his sorrows and fears. Then he comes away with a joyful face. Do you find that you can come away from prayer and not look sad? When Hannah had been at prayer her face was not sad anymore (I Samuel 1:18), she was comforted. This is the right way to contentment.

# Chapter 3 - How Christ Teaches Contentment

A Christian moving toward contentment is a student in Christ's school. The lessons Christ teaches are these:

## The lesson of self-denial

This is a hard lesson. The martyr Bradford said, "Whoever has not learned the lesson of the cross, has not learned the ABC in Christianity." Like children starting elementary school, we begin with this. If you mean to be a Christian at all, you must buckle down to this lesson of self-denial. It humbles and softens a man's heart. Strike something soft and it makes no noise, but strike something hard and it makes a noise. So it is with the hearts of those who are full of themselves and hardened with self-love: if they are tapped, they make a noise. But a self-denying Christian yields to God's hand and makes no noise. Below are several aspects of this lesson of self-denial.

*Such a person learns to know that he is nothing.* He becomes able to say, "Well, I see I am nothing in myself." Learn this thoroughly and you will be able to bear anything. Keep in mind however that, although you are nothing, God gives you his heart by his free grace.

*I deserve nothing.* Suppose I lack this or that which others have? I am sure that I deserve nothing but to be in hell! You say to your discontented employee, "I wonder what you think you deserve?" Or to your child: "Do you deserve it that you are so eager to have it?" You silence them that way, and so we may easily silence ourselves. We deserve nothing, and so why should we be so impatient to get what we want?

*I can do nothing.* Jesus said, "Apart from Me you can do nothing." Why should I be troubled that I do not have this or that, when the truth

36

is that I can do nothing? Suppose you meet someone who is angry because he does not have just the sort of meals he wants. You might say to him, "I wonder what work you do or what use you are?" Should someone who sits around useless have a steady supply of whatever he wants? If you consider what little need God has of you, it will limit your discontentment. If you have learned this lesson of self-denial then, though God shorts you on some comforts, you will say, "Since I do so little, why should I have a lot?" This thought will bring down a man's spirit as much as anything.

*I am so wicked that without God's help I cannot receive anything good.* I am not only an empty vessel but a corrupt and unclean vessel that would spoil anything put into it. So are all our hearts. Every one of them is not only empty of good but is like a musty bottle that spoils even good liquid that is poured into it.

*If God cleanses us to a degree by giving us some grace of his Spirit, still we can make no use of it if God withdraws himself.* What if he leaves us a moment after giving us the greatest gifts and abilities? He might say, "I will give you these things; now go and do business with them—and without me." We cannot progress one foot farther if he leaves us. How disgustingly we would abuse those gifts and abilities!

*We are worse than nothing.* By sin we become a good deal worse than nothing and contrary to all good. We are not empty pitchers in respect to good but are like pitchers filled with poison. So is it so scandalous that people like us are shorted on outward comforts?

Put these seven things together and then Christ has taught you self-denial. A man who is little in his own eyes will account every hardship as small and every mercy as great. Consider King Saul. When he was little in his own eyes, his hardships seemed light to him and he stayed humble. But later, when some did not want him to be king but spoke contemptuously of him, he began to be a big man in his own eyes. Then his hardships began to feel heavy to him.

No one is so contented as a self-denying man or woman. No one ever denied himself as much as Jesus did, who gave his cheek to the smiters, opened not his mouth, and was a lamb led to the slaughter. He denied himself more than anyone ever did and was willing to empty himself, and so he was the most contented person that ever lived. The nearer we come to learning to deny ourselves as he did, the more contented we shall be; and by fully acknowledging our own wickedness, we will learn to justify whatever God does.

For God is just and righteous to lay any burden on us since he is dealing with such wretched creatures. A discontented person is troubled for lack of comfort, but a self-denying person thinks it a wonder that he has as much comfort as he has. He wonders why God gives him liberty to breathe, considering how wicked and sinful the Lord sees him to be.

One thing more about self-denial that brings contentment: *the soul comes to rejoice and find satisfaction in all God's ways.* A selfish man will be glad about whatever suits his own goals, but a godly and self-denying man about everything that suits God's goals. He says, "God's goals are my goals and I've denied my own goals." So his comforts are multiplied, not being limited to what he alone wants. If you wait till God's goals happen to coincide with yours, you will only be content now and then.

Because people battle among themselves so selfishly, they are like those who jostle and fight one another to get through a narrow street. But those with large hearts, who make public things their goals and can deny themselves, have room to walk without such jostling.

### The vanity of created things

Whatever is created has an emptiness to it. "Vanity of vanities! All is vanity" (Ecclesiastes 1:2), is what Solomon learned: creation of itself does us neither good nor harm; it is all like a wind. Nothing in creation is suitable for a godly person to feed on for good and happiness. The reason you are disappointed by the things of the world is not because you have not accumulated enough of them. Rather it is because they are not in proportion to that immortal soul of yours that is capable of appreciating God himself. Many think they are unhappy because they do not have enough of the things of this world, but having more would not satisfy them. They are like a hungry man who tries to swallow the wind and who then thinks he is not satisfied because he has not gotten enough of it! "Why do you spend money for what is not bread, and your wages for what does not satisfy? (Isaiah 55:2). Are you crazy? Riches say, "Contentment is not in me";

pleasure says, "Contentment is not in me"; all created things say the same. Contentment is higher than that.

## The one thing necessary

You know that Jesus told Martha, who had many cares and concerns, that there is just one thing necessary (Luke 10:38-42). It is not necessary for me to be rich, but I must make peace with God; it is not necessary that I should live a life of pleasure, but it is absolutely necessary that I have pardon for my sin; it is not necessary that I have honor or promotion, but I must have God, I must have Jesus, I must have my soul saved. I may have the other fine things—a good house, plenty of income, fashionable clothes, and career advancement—but what if I then perish forever? No matter how poor I may be, I may have this absolute necessity. If Christ causes the fear of eternity to come upon you, then it possesses your heart and draws you away from the things of this world.

When Pompey was bringing corn to Rome at a time of scarcity, he was in great danger of storms at sea. "We must go on," he said, "It is necessary that Rome should be relieved, but it is not necessary that we should live." So we too should not trouble our souls about lesser matters. What disquiets us here in this world but some side issues? That is because our hearts are not taken up with the one absolutely necessary thing.

Who are more discontented than idle people, those with nothing to occupy their minds? Every little thing disturbs them. But a man who has business of great weight and consequence, if the business goes well, is not even aware of small family matters. On the other hand, a man who sits around home with nothing to do finds fault with everything. In the same way, when a man has nothing to do but to be busy about creature comforts, every little thing troubles him; but when a man is taken up with the weighty things of eternal life, matters of this world are of comparatively little consequence to him.

**The soul understands what relationship it has to the world.**

While I live in the world I am just a stranger here, a traveler, and a soldier. When a man is at home he is not content unless things are just so. A man on a trip however may put up with a strange diet and a lumpy bed without getting upset. He reminds himself that he is in another man's house, and though things are not like home, it would be bad manners to complain.

Similarly, travellers have to be content with bad weather. If rain were pouring in a man's roof at home, he would call it intolerable, but he puts up with it on a trip. Sailors at sea wear any old clothes and may eat nothing but salt meat, yet they are content. They know that when the voyage is over they will wear fine suits and dine as they please. We are in this world like seafaring men, tossed on the waves. Our destination and haven is heaven. Though our diet is poor, we should not let it grieve us. "Beloved, I urged you as aliens and strangers to abstain from fleshly lusts which wage war against the soul" (I Peter 2:11).

So do not plan to satisfy yourselves here. When a man comes into an inn and sees there a cupboard full of fine silver plate, he is not troubled that he does not own it. Why? Because he is going away. So let us not be troubled when we see others with great wealth. Why? Because we are going to another country. You are, so to speak, spending just the night here in this world. Even if you were to live a hundred years, in comparison to eternity it is not as much as one night; it is as though you were traveling and had come to an inn. What madness, then, for a man to be discontented because he does not have what he sees there at the inn, considering he will be going away again in just a short time.

David wrote, "I am a stranger in the earth; do not hide your commandments from me" (Psalm 119:19). Since he is a traveler through this world, he says God's commandments are enough for him, the rules to guide his life by.

"Suffer hardship with me, as a good soldier of Christ Jesus" (II Timothy 2:3), Paul wrote to Timothy. When a soldier is away from his warm bed at home, he sometimes has to lie on straw, but he thinks to himself, "This is only what a soldier has to expect." How shameful if a soldier were to go whining with tears in his eyes, complaining that he does not have steak at every meal and sleep in a pre-warmed bed! Christians who are warriors against the enemies of their souls must also be willing to endure hard conditions. Especially when they consider that they are guaranteed final victory and the end of all sorrows, they should be content.

### The good that can be enjoyed from anything God has created

There is some goodness in the things of this world, some desirableness, but it is not in the things themselves but in how they relate to God. Use of them may draw me nearer to God, so that I may enjoy more of him and be of more service for his glory. On the other hand, if I do not enjoy God in something, there is no goodness in it.

Suppose that a man has lost his wealth. I would ask the man, "When you had your wealth, what good did it do you?" A godless man would reply, "Everyone knows the answer to that. It brought me so much income a year, the best food, a fine reputation, regard from others for my opinions, any clothing I wanted, and inheritances prepared for my kids." This man does not know what the true value of his estate was! So no wonder that he is dejected when he loses it. Asked the same question, a wise Christian would reply, "Wealth gave me the opportunity to serve God better, to do a great deal of good for others, and so show them something of God's goodness. Now that the money is gone, if God will allow me to demonstrate his goodness just as much through my sufferings, then I will be as content as I was before."

Suppose God calls you away from prosperity, saying, "I will have you honor me in a suffering condition instead." That is how you honor God, when you can turn this way or that, to whatever he calls you. Though impoverished, essentially you have the same good as before.

### Knowledge of our own hearts

prov. 4:23

Even if you are illiterate, God expects you to read your heart. It will help you to contentment in three ways:

*You will discover the root of your discontentment.* Many are mistaken about the cause of their discontentment, which is always

41

some corruption and disorder of the heart. When we have studied our hearts enough to know them well, and we are discontent, then like a watch repairer we will be able to find the cause and fix it.

*You will know what best suits your situation in life.* Until you understand your heart, you will not give a thought to the need you have for troubles. But one who knows his heart can say, "I would not have missed this trouble for anything. If not for it I would have fallen into sin." An uneducated man thinks the emetic the doctor gave him will kill him, but if a doctor takes a purge and then is violently sick from it, he is all the more pleased with the effect. He knows it will help to make him well. So we would be pleased by our troubles if we only could understand the diseases of our spirits. We must give the cure a chance to work.

*They know what they are able to manage.* Some who know their hearts well will admit they cannot manage much wealth and prosperity. This is like a wise farmer who will not have herds so large that they overgraze his available land. In contrast, do not be like the little girl who wept because she wanted a coat as long as the one worn by her twenty year old sister. Or do not be like a child who wants you to give it a knife to play with. We would not cry for some things if we knew what it would be like to have them. Cecolampadius said of his extreme poverty, "Though I have been very poor, yet I would be poorer." What he meant was, "The Lord knew that a poor condition was more suitable for me than to be rich."

### The burden of prosperity

Prosperity is quite a burden and it requires great strength to bear it. Many see the shine and glitter of prosperity who do not see the burden. Actually, it is a fourfold burden:

*A burden of trouble.* The Bible says that those who want to be rich pierce themselves with many griefs (I Timothy 6:10). Their delusion is like someone who sees a town from far off that looks lovely to him, but when he comes into the town it is all dirty lanes and potholes. In the same way, we admire the prosperity of some rich man, but if we only knew his troubles with family, possessions, and business dealings, we would see a different picture. A man may wear a fine

42

new shoe, but only he knows where it pinches him. Do not assume that the rich are happier than you are.

*A burden of danger.* Prosperous people are often in danger. They may be like moths to the flame, for they are subject to many temptations that most people never know. Tall trees are broken by storms more than low shrubs, and it is the ship with all its sails up that is in the most danger from a gale. You know that the Bible says how hard it is for rich men to get into heaven. So be content as you are!

Some of the Biblical tribe of Levi were the Kohathites. They were honored above the other priestly families by being chosen to give service in the Tabernacle with the most holy things of all, and were also honored in other ways, but it came with a price. When the Israelites traveled, the other Levites got to carry their gear on ox-drawn wagons, but the Kohathites had to carry theirs on their shoulders! This pictures how those in honor even nowadays have burdens that those under them do not know about. Many a minister or judge lies awake while you sleep. If you knew their burdens, you would consider yours light by comparison.

Though their ministry was in the very Holy of Holies in the Tabernacle, the Kohathites were warned not to go in and see the holy things more than was called for in God's instructions. It was as much as their lives were worth! Do anything beyond their strictly limited duties, and they would die. So though they were honored, they were in more danger. Similarly, ministers nowadays are on the receiving end of all the spite and malice of ungodly men. Though God employs them in a service that even angels would delight in, yet their burden of danger is all the greater.

So be content.

*A burden of responsibility.* You see only the sweetness, comfort, honor, and respect that people in prosperous positions have, but you ought to consider the greater duty they owe to God. You covet the honor, but can you carry the burden of responsibility?

*A burden of accountability.* The less you have, the less you will be accountable for to God. So your account in comparison to a minister's or a judge's is small: perhaps no more than your own soul and some responsibility for your family. Those in higher positions must be accountable for congregations, towns, cities, and even whole countries.

You daydream about the glories of kings! But what if you were one and were held accountable for all the disorder and wickedness of a kingdom, things which you might have prevented? What great glory a king might bring to God by painstakingly honoring him in a kingdom! Whatever God loses through the king's lack of such effort, that king must give an account for. Chrysostom wondered that any man in public service can be saved for heaven, because the account they have to give is so great.

Philip, the King of Spain, had such a strong conscience that he, as the story goes, said he would not go against it—even in secret—even to gain the whole world. Yet when he came to die, he cried out, "Oh, that I had never been a king! Oh, that I had lived a solitary and private life all my days! Then I would have died much more securely, I would have gone with more confidence before the throne of God to give my account. This is the fruit of my kingdom: because I had days of glory in it, it has made my account harder to give to God."

So you who are in humble positions remember this. Latimer said in one of his sermons, "The half is more than the whole." Halfway toward the dizzy heights of prosperity, he meant, is safer. Those in a high and prosperous condition are chained to the burdens of trouble, danger, responsibility, and accountability.

**The dreadful evil of being allowed to have your own way**

If God abandons you by allowing you your desires, it is surely the most hideous and fearful calamity that can happen to anyone on the face of the earth. It is a spiritual judgment more frightening than any external judgment. Once you understand this, you will be content when God crosses you, denying you anything you want. Instead you become all vexed and upset about it! Well, is that your only misery, to be crossed in your desires? No, no, you are completely mistaken. The greatest misery of all is for God to give you up to your own lusts, to your own plans.

Psalm 81:11-12 has it: "But My people did not listen to My voice, and Israel did not obey me." What then? "So I gave them over to the stubbornness of their heart, to walk in their own devices." Bernard commented, "Oh let me not have such a misery as that! For to give

44

me what I would have, to give me my heart's desires is one of the most hideous judgments in the world."

In the Bible a near certain sign of a reprobate is for God to give the man up to his own desires. All the pain of diseases, all the calamities that can be imagined are no judgments at all in comparison to this. So why be so troubled when you do not have your own way? The Lord sends the plague of his curse through prosperity. Uzziah, though a king, had from God the plague of leprosy, and what poor but healthy man in his kingdom would have changed places with him? Better to be dressed in rags than to wear satin and velvet and be a leper. Though, in contrast to Uzziah's fate, God's curse of allowing you your own way may be spiritual only, yet spiritual judgments are the heaviest of all, even worse than leprosy.

The Lord may take away my wealth, but what if it had been my health? At a higher level, ask this: what is my health compared to my soul? If God's judgments on you are merely external things, such as affect your wallet or your digestion, then at least he has not given up on you. He has not given you over to the hardness of your heart or taken away the spirit of prayer from you. Whatever your external misfortunes, you should feel relieved that your soul is not harmed. Thank the Lord that you do not have the plague of a hard heart.

### The correct understanding of God's providence

There are four points to be made:

*The universality of providence.* This refers to how God's providence extends to everything in the world, reaching to every detail of our individual lives. Not a hair falls from your head, not a sparrow to the ground, except by the providence of God, and this extends to all things good or evil. All day every day nothing happens to you unless God's hand is in it. This consideration will help you to be content, especially if you combine your knowledge of it with faith.

*The effectiveness of providence.* The providence of God operates in everything, with strength and power, and will not be changed by us. Fret and rage as you will, yet you will not change the course of providence in the slightest. Job's friends said to him, "For your sake

45

is the earth to be abandoned, or the rock to be moved from its place?" (Job 18:4).

So I may say to every malcontent: "What? Shall the providence of God change its course for you? Do you think it so weak that, because of your displeasure, it will change its course? It will go on regardless, with the power to carry everything before it. Will your fits of emotion make one hair black or white? If you were on a swiftly sailing ship, could you make it stand still by running back and forth on the deck? Well, that's how much you can affect the providence of God, do what you will."

*The infinite variety of the works of providence, kept in order.* God's infinite works interact in an orderly way. In his providence a thousand, thousand things depend on one another. All God's works from all eternity are like an infinite number of wheels making up a single unified mechanism, and in their orderly motion they achieve the end that he appointed from all eternity.

Like a child staring at clockworks, we can only see things one piece at a time and do not consider their relationship. God sees all things at once and their interrelation.

Notice how this affects our contentment. When something happens to me, that is one wheel in the clock, and it may be that if that one wheel were stopped it would stop all the other wheels, dependent as they are on each other. So when God has ordered something to happen, how do you know how many other things depend on it? He may have some work to do twenty years from now that depends on that bit of providence that happens today or this week.

So 'all you want' is one little change in providence? By itself it would amount to so little! But by wanting your own way in this detail, you may cross God in a thousand things that he has to bring about, because the thousand things may depend on that detail. Stop one wheel and the clock stops. If you love God, be willing to be crossed in a few things so that he may work on in general toward a thousand things.

*Knowing God's usual way of dealing with his people.* We often think God's providences are strange and troublesome and do not know what to make of them. This comes from not being used to the usual way God handles his people. Like newcomers to a household or new employees at a company, we just need to give ourselves time to see

46

why the old hands do things in their peculiar ways. The following are the three things about God's ways that we need to get to know.

First, God's ordinary course is that his people in this world should suffer hardships. This is all the more true since the gospel came into the world. Those who do not understand wonder how it can be that the godly are troubled, wounded, and despoiled while their enemies triumph. Yet this is God's will and God's way. Therefore the apostle wrote, "Beloved, do not be surprised at the fiery ordeal among you" I Peter 4:12.

Second, usually when God intends the greatest blessing for his people, he first brings them into the lowest condition. If it is a bodily or external blessing he has in mind, he first brings them low physically or outwardly. If it is a matter of possessions, he takes them away and then restores them. He may lower his people's reputations, or perhaps their spirits, before raising them. Now those who are ignorant may view every such lowering as God abandoning and forsaking his people, or at least that he means them little good. But a child of God is not troubled. He remembers that, when God intended to raise Joseph to be second in command over Egypt, he first cast him into a dungeon. When the Lord wanted to set David on a throne, he first made him to be hunted like a quail by his enemies.

God even dealt this way with his Son. Christ himself ascended to glory by the path of suffering; and if God dealt with his own Son that way, how much more with his people! It is always darkest before the dawn. Before God granted our army such great mercy at the Battle of Naseby, it looked dark for us.

Third, God's way is to work by contraries, turning evil into good. Not only does he grant good after evil, he even turns evil into good. Luther said, "It is the way of God: he humbles that he might exalt, he kills that he might make alive, he confounds that he might glorify." The deepest wisdom tells us that God, when he wants to bring us life, brings it out of death. He brings joy out of sorrow, prosperity out of adversity, and many times brings grace out of sin, that is, he makes use of sin to promote grace. God brings good out of evil, not only to overcome the evil but to make it work toward what is good. Understanding this should put an end to our complaining and bring contentment to our spirits, but I fear that only a few really do understand. Most have not learned it from Jesus.

## Chapter 4 - The Excellence of Contentment

E ven the heathen philosophers had a glimpse of the high value of contentment. Antisthenes asked his gods for nothing to make his life happy but contentment. He asked them for the spirit of Socrates, to be able to bear any wrong or injury and to continue in a calm spirit, so that nobody could notice any change in him. If a pagan, having nothing to work with but his willpower, could appreciate contentment that much, then how much more should we Christians appreciate it! In this chapter I intend to show you the tremendous value of contentment, so that you will be in love with it.

### By contentment we give God his proper worship.

By practicing contentment we give God a special portion of the worship we owe him, and we show proper respect for him. We ought to lie down before him as a dog does before his master, and in what frame of mind could we do it better than when we are content with whatever he brings us? This is to be like the poor woman of Canaan who begged of Jesus that, like a dog, she might have just a few crumbs of his grace, like crumbs fallen from a table. When you can say, "Lord, I'm like a dog, but let me have a crumb," you highly honor God and greatly worship him.

You worship God more by this than when you hear a sermon, spend an hour in prayer, or receive sacraments. For all your hearing, praying, and receiving will not be honored by God if you are discontent. Rather he wants to have your soul's worship as you subject yourself to him. Though in *active* obedience we worship God by doing what pleases him, yet by *passive* obedience we worship him

49

just as well by being pleased with whatever he does. So when doing things for God, a Christian says, "Oh, I hope I can do what pleases God!" But when it comes to any trial, "Oh, I want to be pleased by whatever God does!" What a Christian he is who practices both of these! That is a complete Christian.

**When we are content we receive more grace.**

I divide this into the headings of variety of graces, strength of grace, and beauty of grace.

*Variety of graces.* In contentment there is, as it were, a pharmacist's compound of grace consisting of faith, humility, love, patience, wisdom, and hope. The oil of the compound has all these as its ingredients. In contentment you have them all! God sees these graces of his Spirit in use, and it pleases his heart.

*Strength of grace.* It takes a very sturdy body to endure hard weather, whatever comes, and not be much affected. So it implies strength of grace to be content. Though your memory may be faulty and your abilities poor, do you nevertheless have this gift of heart contentment? If you do, then you have strength of grace.

If a man's body is riddled with illnesses but his mind is still sharp, that implies great strength of brain. So it is with a man's spirit. If his spirit is weak, you will soon find him out of temper. Others who encounter similar trials still keep on steadily, making use of reason and God's graces, and possess their souls in patience.

Though other birds cry out when they are hungry, it is said of the eagle that it endures hunger silently. It is above hunger and thirst! In a similar way some of us, whatever happens, do not whine and complain but go on steadily and thank God. Such men and women, when they meet with what causes others to be dejected and comfortless, do not change at all in their spirits.

*Beauty of Grace.* Seneca said, "When you go out into groves and woods, and see the tallness of the trees and their shadows, it strikes a kind of awful fear of a deity in you, and when you see the vast rivers and fountains of deep waters, that strikes a kind of fear of a god in you, but do you see a man who is quiet in tempests, and who lives happily in the midst of adversities, why do not you worship that man?" He considers a man worthy of such honor who will be quiet and live a

50

happy life, though in the midst of adversities. The glory of God appears more in such a man than in his works of creation: sun, moon, stars, and the whole world.

That was what convinced the Babylonian King Nebuchadnezzar that the God of Israel was truly the great God: when he saw the three children of Israel could walk about in the fiery furnace and not be harmed (Daniel 3). So it is when a Christian can walk in the midst of fiery trials without his clothes being singed, and has comfort and joy through it all. One also thinks of how the jailor was affected when Paul sang in the stocks (Acts 16:23-25). Men will be convinced when they see the power of grace in the midst of adversity. This is the glory of a Christian.

It was the glory of Christ. Bible scholars say that Micah 5:5 speaks of Jesus prophetically when it says that a man will be our peace when the Assyrian invades the land and occupies our palaces. To be at peace when there are no enemies around is no great thing, but this verse says the man will be at peace even when his homeland is conquered. That is, when everyone is in a hubbub and uproar, yet this man shall be our peace.

You may think you have peace in Christ when you have no outward troubles, but is he your peace when the enemy comes? Suppose you should hear the tramp of enemy soldiers marching into your town, and suppose they have broken past all defenses and are plundering? What would be your peace then? Jesus may be peace to the soul when the invaders enter the city and even your houses. If any of you have been through such an invasion, how peaceful were your souls? The grace of contentment will sustain you even when the Assyrian enters the land.

**Contentment prepares the soul to receive mercy.**

None in the world are so prepared to receive grace as those who have contented spirits. You have to hold a container still to pour liquid into it. So, if we want to be vessels that receive God's mercy, we must have quiet, still hearts. If a child throws a fit about wanting something, you do not give it to him until he gets quiet. You wait till he comes and stands still before you and is contented without it, and then you give it to him. Like a child, as soon as you want something

51

from the Lord, you are immediately in an uproar in your spirit. God intends mercy to you, but he says, "I'll see you quiet first, and then come to me and we'll see about it."

Is not this your own experience? Maybe you were troubled and upset because of the lack of some spiritual comfort and got nothing from God for a long while. Then you calmed yourself and could say, "Well, it's right for the Lord to do what he wants with us poor creatures. I'm under his feet and am resolved to do what I can to honor him, regardless of what he does with me. I'll seek God as long as I live; I'll be content with what he gives; and whether he gives or not I'll be content." Then God says, "Now you shall have comfort and mercy."

A prisoner must not think he can be rid of his chains by pulling and yanking; he may bruise his flesh and even cut himself to the bone, but it will not get him free a moment sooner. If he wants his fetters off, he must quietly submit to someone with the key. If a beggar knocks at your door and, when you do not come, becomes vexed and angry about it, blaming you out loud for keeping him standing there; then you will not give him a penny. But suppose you hear a couple of beggars at your door saying, "Let's wait patiently. Maybe they're busy. After all, it's a mercy if we get anything here finally. We don't deserve a thing, so let's wait a while." You would then quickly give them a handout.

So God deals with us.

### Contentment prepares the soul to serve God.

If a man will serve God, he must have a steady heart. So when the Lord has some great work for one of his servants to do, usually he first quiets the man's spirit. Once the servant is contented with anything that comes, the Lord releases him to do the work.

### Contentment delivers us from many temptations.

Oh, the temptations that malcontents are subject to! The devil loves to fish in troubled waters, that is, where he sees people troubled and vexed. To such people he says, "Will you put up with a life like yours? How poor you are! While others are well off, you don't know

52

what to do to get through the winter, to pay the heating bill, or to buy food for you and your kids. Try this trick, this indirect way." And so he tempts them to do something illegal.

By exploiting people's discontent, the devil has persuaded some to even give their souls to him. Melancholy, disgruntled people listen to his promises of wealth and of revenge on their enemies, and so they take up witchcraft. That is their road to contentment. What opportunities for temptation the devil has when he comes across a discontented person!

Luther said, "God does not dwell in Babylon, but in Salem." Babylon signifies confusion, and Salem signifies peace. So this means God does not dwell in spirits that are in confusion but in peaceful, quiet spirits. God's peace guards the heart from temptation.

The story is told of one Marius Curio who had bribes sent to him to tempt him to be a traitor to his country. They came and promised him rewards while he was sitting at home at a dinner that was no more than a dish of turnips. He said, "That man who can be contented with the food that I have will not be tempted with your rewards. I thank God I am content with this food, and as for rewards, let them be offered to those that cannot be content to dine on a dish of turnips."

The truth is that the reason many betray their trust in the service of Parliament and the Kingdom is because they cannot stand to be underpaid and poorly clothed. But a contented man is armored against thousands of the devil's temptations. Those same temptations succeed against others so that their souls are damned.

In times like these, when men are in danger of losing their houses and savings, those without this grace of contentment are in a sorry state. But actually the danger to their souls is worse than the danger to their possessions. You think it so sad that you might lose everything you own in a single night; but if you have a discontented spirit, you are in more danger than that. The devil may plunder you of all that is *lastingly* good by leading you into sin. When men think they must live in all the elegance they used to enjoy, they make themselves a prey to the devil. But some can say, "Let God do with me whatever he pleases. I'm content to submit to him." The devil hardly dares to approach such men.

Once there was a philosopher who lived on poor food. As he was eating herbs and roots, someone said to him, "If you would only try to please King Dionysius, you wouldn't have to eat herbs and roots." He answered, "If you would just be content with poor food, you wouldn't need to flatter King Dionysius." Temptations will have no more effect on a contented man than a dart thrown against a bronze wall.

**Contentment brings abundant comforts into your life.**

Nothing makes a man's life so sweet and comfortable as the grace of contentment. I will demonstrate this in several ways.

*Whatever a man has is his with a sort of independency*, because he does not rely on anyone or anything on earth to supply him with comfort.

*If God raises a contented man to a higher worldly position, he has the love of God with it.* It is far sweeter than if he were to have the promotion and be discontented. For though God may grant the desire of a discontented man, he does not do it from love.

*Contentment provides steady, reliable comforts to the soul.* It keeps on burning like a ship's lantern at sea, no matter what storms or tempests may come.

**Contentment draws comfort even from things we do not possess.**

Many people who lack material things have more comfort than those who have them. Compare it to a man whose job is distilling herbs. Though he does not own the herbs, yet because he is working over them he inhales their aromas and gets their medicinal benefits. Similarly, though a man is far from wealthy, yet by the grace of contentment he may get the comfort of a wealthy condition.

In Plutarch we read of how Sineus came to King Pyrrhus and tried to persuade him to stop making war against the Romans.

He said to the king, "May it please your Majesty, it's reported that the Romans are very good men of war, and if it please the gods that we overcome them, what benefit shall we have of the victory?"

Pyrrhus answered him, "We shall then straightway conquer all the rest of Italy with ease."

54

"Indeed that's likely which your Grace speaks," said Sineus, "but when we have won Italy, will our wars end then?"

"If the gods were pleased that the victory were achieved," said Pyrrhus, "the way would then be made open for us to attain great conquests, for who would not afterwards go into Africa, and so to Carthage?"

"But," said Sineus, "when we have everything in our hands what shall we do in the end?"

Then Pyrrhus, laughing, told him, "We will then be quiet, and take our ease, and have feasts every day, and be as merry with one another as we possibly can."

Said Sineus, "What prevents us now from being quiet and merry together, since we enjoy that immediately without further travel and trouble which we would seek for abroad, with such shedding of blood and manifest danger? Can you not sit down and be merry now?"

So a man may think, "If I had a certain something, then I would get another, and if I had that, then I would get more." And what if you get all your desire? Then you would be content. But why go at it that way? You may be content now without all that. Certainly, our contentment is not obtained by getting what we desire but in God tailoring our spirits to our situations. Some men do not own a square foot of land, but they live better than others who are heirs to plenty of acres and yet are financially embarrassed. Sometimes a sharecropper, by care and hard work, lives better than another man who owns his own land. Many, by this art of contentment, may live better without property than others do who own property.

You will find more comfort in contentment than in any amount of possessions. In fact, a man will have more comfort in being content without something than he would by having it, that is, by having it and being discontent. I shall show this in several ways:

*Surely it is better to be content because of God's grace in my soul than because of some external comfort?*

*If I were to get the thing I want, it would not make my soul better.* But by contentment my soul is better. Neither wealth, nor lands, nor friends will make me a better person.

*If I achieve contentment by satisfying my desire, that is only self-love*, but when I am contented with the will of God, and am ready to do his will, that comes from my love for God.

*If I get something I want, maybe I will be contented about that one thing, but it does not help me to be contented about something else.* Maybe I will be all the more irritable and demanding about other things! But if I have once overcome my heart and am content by God's grace, it makes me content not only about that one matter but in general, accepting whatever happens to me.

So you see that contentment fills a man's life with comfort in this world. The truth is, it is virtually heaven on earth. For what is heaven but the rest and quiet in a man's spirit? What makes heaven to be heaven is the rest and joy there and the satisfaction in God. Well, that is what is in a contented spirit: rest, joy, and satisfaction in God. In heaven praises are sung to God, and likewise a contented heart is always praising and blessing him.

You have heaven on earth when you have a contented spirit; yes, in some regards it is even better than heaven. How so? The heavenliness of contentment on earth has a sort of honor and excellence in God's eyes that contentment in heaven above does not. You see, in heaven there are no temptations to be overcome. There they are not tried by any misfortunes. Though they receive the benefit of God's grace, they have nothing but encouragement to do so (and truly their experience of grace there is perfect, and in that they do excel us). But there is nothing to oppose their bliss; they have no trials at all to tempt them to be contrary. Contrast this with a Christian on this earth who, in the midst of adversity, temptations, and troubles, still reaches out to God's grace. He is satisfied with God, Christ, and the Bible's promises, right in the midst of all he suffers. This is an honor God receives from us that he does not appear to have from the angels and saints in heaven. God will not have that kind of glory from you after you reach heaven. So do not yearn so much to be released from your troubles in this world. Though it would mean more ease for you, it would deny you an invaluable means to honor God, one you can only make use of now.

So, I say, be content with your contentment, for it is a rich gift from the Lord. If he would give you millions of pounds, it would not be such a fortune as this, that he gives you a contented spirit. Say to the Lord, "Though I lack some comforts that others have, you've given me what is as good if not better: a quiet, contented heart that's ready to do what you want."

## Contentment is a great blessing of God to the soul.

God blesses contented people in their possessions, in all they have. In Deuteronomy the Lord blesses the tribe of Judah in this way, saying that they will have all good things sufficient for them. The trick is to enjoy what you have, for even many who are well-off are unable to enjoy their possessions. Only by the blessing of God to your soul will you be able to enjoy life, when he has made your heart's longings even with your circumstances.

## Contented people will be rewarded by God.

God will give us the equivalent good of all the things we are contented to do without. There is some blessing which you think would be very pleasant to you if only you had it. Can you bring your heart to submit to God about it? If so, you will have the blessing one way or the other. If you do not get the thing you wanted, you will have a sort of bill of exchange to receive something in place of it. The substitute will be some reward for your soul.

Here is a comparison. The Bible tells us that God allows one's will to obey him to be a substitute for actually obeying. Though we cannot do some good thing for him, if our hearts are upright and willing, we shall have his blessing. Just as a wicked man will have the punishment for all the sin he wished to commit but could not, so you shall have the reward for good you only hoped to do. Let us apply this principle to passive obedience. Can you be content to lack what others have? Then you shall be no loser. You will have the blessing they have in one way or another, either in this world or the next. With contentment you have all kinds of riches.

**By contentment the soul comes as near as possible to God's excellence.**

The great glory of God is to be happy in his self-sufficiency. In contentment you come near to this. Suppose God were to un-make all creation except for you alone. Having God, you would still be as happy as you are now. Therefore contentment has great excellence.

## Chapter 5 - The Evils of a Grumbling Spirit

Perhaps you feel how far you have been from this grace of contentment which has now been explained to you. Perhaps you have had a grumbling, vexed, and fretful heart. Every little opposition to your will has made you upset and out of temper. What evil God sees in this! I shall attempt, in the headings below, to help you to be humbled, for there is more evil in your attitude than you are aware of.

**Grumbling and discontentedness reveal serious corruption in the soul.**

If every scratch of a pin makes a man's skin fester into a sore, it shows he is seriously diseased. Well, what then if every little trouble makes you grumble? It is not the severity of your misfortune that is making you miserable; the problem is in your soul. So when the misfortune comes you had better ponder the hidden disease of your grumbling heart. Treat the illness inside and not the outward symptom.

**When God describes the wicked he often speaks of their grumbling.**

Consider the 14th and 15th verses of Jude. "It was also about these men that Enoch, in the seventh generation from Adam, prophesied, saying, 'Behold the Lord came with many thousands of his holy ones, to execute judgment upon all, and to convict all the ungodly of all their ungodly deeds which they have done in an ungodly way, and of all the harsh things which ungodly sinners have spoken against Him.'"

Notice how the word 'ungodly' is used four times here! But who exactly are these very ungodly people? The next verse says that, "These are grumblers…" And thousands of punishing angels are after them! Look to your souls then, and see that this grumbling, the vice opposite to contentment, is not so minor a matter as you think. You think you are not so ungodly as others because you do not swear and drink as they do, but you may be ungodly in grumbling. It is true that even the godly have some seeds and remainders of various sins within them. Nevertheless, men who are under the power of this sin of grumbling are just as certainly ungodly as if they were drunkards or adulterers.

### God accounts grumbling as rebellion.

Grumbling is contrary to the worship of God. A grumbling heart is a rebellious heart. Numbers 16:41 says, "But on the next day all the congregation of the sons of Israel grumbled against Moses and Aaron, saying, 'You are the ones who have caused the death of the Lord's people.'" Compare this with chapter 17, verse 10: "But the Lord said to Moses, 'Put back the rod of Aaron before the testimony to be kept as a sign against the *rebels*…'" So you see that to be a grumbler is to be a rebel against God.

When a rebellion is brewing in any earthly kingdom, it begins with grumbling from house to house. It is like the smoke and smoldering before a fire breaks out. So because grumbling has the seed of rebellion in it, the Lord accounts it to be rebellion. So if you are guilty of the sin of grumbling, accuse your wretched heart of being guilty of rebellion against God. Humble your soul.

### Grumbling discontent is flatly opposed to God's grace, especially to his bringing the soul home to heaven.

Nothing is more contrary to God's conversion of sinners.

This can be shown by reviewing the work of God when he brings a sinner home to himself:

*When God brings a sinner to himself, the usual way is for him to make the soul see the evil that is in sin.* He wants the sinner to be sensible of the wide breach that sin makes between God and himself. Certainly, Jesus can never be known in his beauty and excellence until the sinner knows this. Whatever other works God may do in the soul, the man must at least recognize the evil of sin and the excellence of Jesus Christ.

But just think how contrary grumbling is to any such work of God! Do I recognize the evil of sin as the greatest of burdens? Then how can I be so troubled about my every little problem? Certainly, if I see sin's evil, that sight should swallow up all other evils; if I am burdened with sin's evil, that burden should swallow up all others. You ought to say, "What! Am I grumbling against God's will? Just a short time ago the Lord made me see myself as a damned wretch, and made me think it amazing that I was not in hell!"

*Such grumbling is directly opposed to an appreciation of the infinite excellence and glory of Christ, and of the gospel.* After God has shown me the infinite excellence of Jesus, a sight worth ten thousand worlds, shall I be grieved by some small trouble?

*God draws our hearts away from creature comforts.* The Lord says, "Your happiness isn't here in this world, your rest isn't here. Your happiness is elsewhere, and your heart needs to be released from all the things here below in this world." How contrary a grumbling heart is to this! Something which is glued to something else cannot be pulled off unless you tear it. So it is a sign that your heart is glued to this world when God tries to pull you free and your heart tears. On the other hand, if God takes anything away from you by means of some adversity, and you can easily part with it, without tearing, that shows your heart is not glued to the world.

*God makes you depend on Jesus for your every good.* Out of free grace, the Lord gives Jesus to me, providing eternal life and salvation from sin, and now my soul depends on him for its every good. Have you done that? If you think you have, then why are you discontented for the lack of some little creature comfort? Is this your faith? Receive Christ as your Lord to rule over you as he pleases.

*You must give yourself up to God in an everlasting covenant.* Have you done this? Then why do you have a fretting, grumbling heart that is so opposed to such surrender? When you have been grumbling, humble your soul.

Yes, you may have been converted to Christ, but conversion is something that must continue all through your life. You must maintain a sense of your sin, the burden of it that is opposed to God's holiness, goodness, and mercy. In the same way, you must continue to appreciate the excellence of Christ, to feel how you are called away from this world to entrust your soul to him. This must be done day by day as you subdue yourself and surrender to God by covenant. Do this daily and you would not have time for grumbling.

## Grumbling and discontent are far below a Christian.

*Grumbling and discontent are below the relations in which you stand,* as detailed below:

They are below the relationship you have with God the Father. Do you not call him Father, and are you not his child? You are a king's child, and yet you let anything trouble you. It is as if a little prince were to burst into tears just from losing a toy. You dishonor your Father, as if to say that he does not have wisdom, power, or mercy enough to provide for you.

Grumbling and discontent are also below the relationship you have with Jesus. The Bible calls Christians the bride of Christ. So are you married to Jesus and yet troubled and discontented? He says to you, "Aren't I worth more to you than the riches and comforts that you are pining for?" Also consider that God has given you his Son, and with him will he not give you everything else? All the riches of a husband are his wife's. Though some husbands are so shockingly neglectful that their wives have to sue for maintenance, certainly Jesus will never deny maintenance to his spouse. He is not the sort to withhold anything from you if he finds you are frowning.

You have an additional relationship with Christ as a member of his body, spiritually speaking. You are bone of his bone and flesh of his flesh.

Jesus is also your elder brother, and so you are a co-heir with him.

Grumbling and discontent are also below the relationship you have with the Holy Spirit. You are the temple of the Holy Spirit, and he is your Comforter.

They are below the relationship you have with the angels. You are united with them, because Jesus has joined them with his church. They are ministering spirits to supply your needs; and you and they are joined together; and Christ is the head of both.

Grumbling and discontent are below the relationship you have with other Christians. They and you make up one spiritual body with Jesus, and if they are happy, then it follows that you too should be happy.

*Grumbling and discontentedness are below the high dignity that God has given a Christian.* Even the lowliest Christian in the world has the standing of a lord of heaven and earth, of life and death! This is because Christ, as Lord over everything, has made those who are united with him to be lords over everything. Thus even life and death belong to Christians in the sense that faith makes them lords over all, so that even death itself becomes their slave. You are lifted up in excellence above all creatures except the angels, and in some respects even above them. I mean that you have a union with Christ that they do not have, that he died for you and not for them, and that you are a better demonstration of what God can do to raise up one of his creatures and make him happy.

And yet you are discontented, you who were like kindling for hell and who might have been scorching, yelling, and roaring there to all eternity! So will every misfortune be able to say to you, "Bow down to me?" We called it slavery when cruel bishops used to tell us to bow down to them, imposing on our consciences. In effect they were saying, "Let your consciences, your very souls, bow down so we may walk on them." Will you then let every misfortune say, "Bow down that I may walk on you?" That is how it is when your heart is overcome with grumbling and discontent. The devil himself prevails on you in this way.

This is so far beneath the happy position to which God has raised a Christian! Will the son of a King let every lowly fellow that comes along tell him to bow down so he can walk on his neck?

*Grumbling is below the spirit of a Christian.* Great men love to see noble spirits in their children, and our great God loves to see noble spirits in us. Since we are one spirit with God the Father, Christ, and the Holy Spirit, we should have a spirit that shows forth their glory, a lion-like spirit. Christ prayed to his Father that not his own will but

God's would be done, and he showed a lion-like spirit in all kinds of hardships, without once grumbling about them.

The heathens of long ago considered a grumbling spirit to be very low and unmanly, so should not a Christian think it an unchristian-like spirit to be overly dejected by any trouble? Grumbling people are like little children during weaning, so headstrong and vexing! They will neither sleep nor let their mothers sleep. Likewise, when God wishes to wean you from some of the world's outward comforts, how fretful and discontented you are!

*Grumbling is below the claims of a Christian.* A Christian claims to be dead to the world and alive to God. He claims that his life is hidden with Christ in God, and that he satisfies himself in God alone. Is this your claim? And yet if you do not get everything you want, you raise a fuss. You are denying your claims.

*Grumbling is below the special grace of faith.* Faith overcomes the world and makes all God's promises ours. But did God ever promise you a life of ease, quiet, and freedom from troubles? No, that is contrary to what you signed up for. God never promised you a rose garden. Your faith gives you no ground to claim an exemption from trials, so why do you call it such evil to suffer under them? But certainly the life you have by faith is enough to content your heart both now and to all eternity.

A Christian should be satisfied with the proper object of his faith, an object high enough to satisfy his soul; and God is enough to satisfy the soul even if it were capable of receiving a thousand times more grace than it can. When you feel ill-used because you do not get things God never promised, you sin against the gospel and the grace of faith.

*Grumbling is below a Christian, because he forgets that he is supported more than others are.* It is one thing to grumble if you can expect no help from God, but a Christian has all the Lord's promises and decrees to strengthen his spirit.

*It is below the expectation that God has of Christians*, for he not only expects them to be patient in hardships, but even to rejoice and triumph in them. When God expects you to rejoice, you have not even gotten so far as contentedness!

*It is below the response God has had from other believers.* Some others have not only been content through small trials but have even triumphed over great ones. They have suffered the plundering of their possessions with joy. Read toward the end of Hebrews 11 to find the faithful responses God has had from his people.

## By grumbling you undo your prayers.

By praying at all you acknowledge God as your Lord and Master and claim to place yourself at his disposal. If you ask for things in prayer and yet reject the Lord's authority over you, then you annul your prayers as fast as you speak them. On the one hand, you come to him as someone who begs for bread at his gates each day; but on the other hand, you feel you must do whatever you want. This is the undoing of the prayers of a Christian.

Is not the Lord's Prayer the pattern Jesus gave us for our prayers? And did Jesus teach us to pray, "Lord give me this much annual income, this quality of clothing, and thus many dishes at my table?" Rather it is, "Give us our bread," showing that you should be content with a little. And do you not have bread to eat? I hope none of my readers lack that!

People will raise objections such as, "What would become of my children if I were to die?" or, "I don't know where I'll get my groceries for next week or how I'll get through the winter." But where did Jesus teach us to pray for provisions for so long a time? Rather he told us to be content if we have bread for today. So when we grumble because we do not have more, we forget our Lord's Prayer, denying God's authority over us.

## Grumbling produces woeful effects.

*First, you waste a lot of time by grumbling and discontent.* Typically, discontented people get lost in their gloomy thoughts for hours at a time, and all in vain! Your time would be better spent in holy meditation, but you waste it on discontented thoughts. You complain that you cannot concentrate on good things; that if you try, and you begin to think about them, soon you are back to worrying. You get away by yourself and endlessly pore over things that feed your dejection. Do consider your loss of time.

*This dejected spirit also makes you unfit for your duties.* A contented man or woman is ready for anything at any time, and fit to seek God at any time. But discontent distracts you from duty, makes you unfit for it. Bad news, losses, and misfortune—oh, how they distract you, to the point that you cannot enjoy communion with God. If you only had a quiet spirit, severe trials would never keep you from the performance of any duty.

*A fit of discontentment causes wicked uprisings of the heart and resolutions of spirit.* These outbursts may be against God or others, and they sometimes take the form of desperate resolutions to resort to unethical means to get what you want. If the Lord had allowed you to do certain things you have imagined while in a discontented fit, what wretched misery you would have brought on yourself! It was a mercy that he stopped you. Just remember some of the shameful things you have imagined doing, and learn to be humble about it

*Discontent also leads to unthankfulness.* The Bible ranks unthankfulness among the great sins. Discontented people, though they receive many mercies from God, are thankful for none of them. How wicked they are to consider his mercies as if they were nothing, and just because they cannot get what they want.

This applies even to spiritual comforts and gifts—nonmaterial things. People who want to be more spiritual may give no thanks to God for the spirituality they do have, counting it as nothing. Do you think God will take this well? Suppose you were to give a friend some money for his business and he were to respond, "What's this? Pocket change is no good to me!" That would be intolerable to you, that he would react like that just because you did not give him as much money as he wanted. It is no different when you say, "All the spiritual things that God has given me are worthless. It's no good to me—just paltry common gifts. What a hypocrite he is to give me counterfeit goods!" You ingrate, these are the precious graces of God's Spirit and worth more than thousands of worlds.

It is the same concerning outward blessings. God has given you health, strength of body, and a living wage; enough to maintain your family. Yet because you pine for something more, you are ready to call all this nothing. You ought to spend some time each day thanking the Lord for all the mercy he has granted you. There is not one of you in the lowest condition but has plenty of blessings to thank God for, and yet discontentedness counts them as nothing.

Luther said, "This is the rhetoric of the Spirit of God, to extenuate evil things, and to amplify good things; if a cross comes, to make the cross but little, but if there is a mercy, to make the mercy great." So when a cross of misfortune comes, the man of God will wonder that it is no worse than it is, and will thank God that it is not worse. If he experiences a mercy, he wonders at God's goodness for granting so much. So all mercies seem to be great and all hardships seem to be small.

The devil does just the opposite, so Luther says: he underrates God's mercies and amplifies evil things. So while a godly man wonders that his cross is not heavier, a wicked man wonders how his can be so heavy. He says, "No one has ever suffered as much as me!" And if there is a mercy, the devil says to him, "Oh, sure this *looks* good, but what is it really? Not that much. And for all that, you still may end up miserable." Thus the rhetoric of the devil belittles God's mercies and magnifies hardships.

There is a striking example of this in Numbers 16:12-13. "Then Moses sent a summons to Dathan and Abiram, the sons of Eliab, but they said, 'We will not come up. Is it not enough that you have brought us up out of a land flowing with milk and honey to have us die in the wilderness, but you would also lord it over us?'" Note how they slighted Canaan, the land they were going to and that God had promised would flow with milk and honey.

But see how discontentedness affected how they spoke. Because they had met with some troubles in the wilderness, why it was meant to slay them! They made their hardship in the wilderness greater than it was—it was meant to kill them. Actually God's purpose was to carry them to the Promised Land of Canaan. Though their deliverance from cruel slavery in Egypt was a great mercy, they made it out to be nothing. They should have thanked God as long as they lived for delivering them out of Egypt.

We are like Dathan and Abiram when we meet with any misfortune concerning our possessions, our taxes, or any trouble. This is especially so if any among you has lived in a place occupied by enemy forces. You are ready to say, "Though we had plenty, we're under hardship now. We were better off before when we had bishops and government officials domineering over us." Beware of the cursed fruit of discontentment! To be unthankful for God's mercies is a serious evil.

*Finally, grumbling causes shiftiness.* Grumblers are likely to give in to the temptation to shift for themselves in sinful, ungodly, and unlawful ways. How many of you have bad consciences about things you did during times of trouble when the pressure was on? If so, discontent was at the bottom of it. You should mortify discontent at the root.

### Grumbling is a foolish sin.

*Grumbling takes away the present comfort of what you have,* because you do not have something else. You do not like to see this in a little child, do you? You give him some food and he complains because you did not give him more. If you do not immediately give him more, in a temper fit he throws down what he does have. Though you may call this foolishness, it is the same way you deal with God. He gives you blessings, but you see others have more blessings than you and so you cry for more. But God does not give you what you want, and because of that you throw away what you have. Is that not foolish? It is unthankfulness.

*All your discontent does not help you a bit.* You do not gain by it. Jesus asked how anyone by worrying can add an inch to his height or make one white hair turn black? Do you think the Lord will come in mercy a second sooner because of your grumbling? Rather, mercy will be put off longer because of it. Although the Lord was about to relieve you, now you shall not have it. If you are about to give something to your child, but you see him upset and fretting because he does not have it yet, you will delay giving it to him. And this is the very reason why many mercies are denied you, because of your discontent. You deprive yourself of what you want by gnawing on your grudging unhappiness. Is that not foolish?

*Discontented people commonly have many foolish attitudes.* The things they say and do are a painful embarrassment. They are so awkward and laughable as to make themselves a shame to themselves and their friends.

*Discontent eats away the goodness and sweetness of a blessing before it comes.* It is like a worm that eats the meat out of a nut, leaving only the shell. It may be that, when God does give the grumbler what he wants, it will have a curse mixed with it, so that he would have been better off not to have had it. Unless the man is first humbled about his discontent, he will get no comfort from the blessing, but it will be an evil to him instead.

Therefore, if I were to have a dear friend who was discontented because of the lack of some comfort, I would pray, "Lord, deny him this thing until you choose to humble him, because if he has it too soon it will come without any blessing." As for yourself, say to the Lord, "If what I so wildly desire were to come to me before I humble myself about it, I could have no comfort from it. It would come as a misfortune to me."

How many things you think would make you happy if you had them! But when you get them, not only do they not make you happy, but they turn out to be the greatest troubles you ever endured. And this is simply because your heart was excessively set on having them.

Think of Rachel who cried that she must have children or die for lack of them. God granted her wish and she died in childbirth. Perhaps you have had a child who was sick, and you were grumblingly upset with God for fear of losing it. God restores the child to health but maybe makes that child an anguish to your heart all the days of your life.

Someone said about the manna, which was miraculously granted as food to the Israelites, "When the people were contented with this manna God gave them, then it was very good, but as soon as they tried to gather more of it than God had told them to, then, the Bible says, it became infested with worms." So when we are content with what God gives, we get the sweet blessing, but if we insist on more or to keep it longer than God wants us to have it, then there will be worms in it, it will be no good at all.

*Grumbling makes a hardship much worse than it might have been.* Far from removing our misfortunes, grumbling makes them worse. Why? Because a discontented heart is a proud heart, and a proud heart will not lower sails when a storm comes. If a sea captain, when a storm comes, is stiff-necked and refuses to lower sails, he only makes things worse. So it is with the pride of a discontented man who will not pull down his spirit at all or bow to God about the storm of some hardship. It is a thousand to one that the tempest will overwhelm his soul.

**Discontent is very dangerous, for it provokes God's wrath.**

Consider Numbers 14:26: "The Lord spoke to Moses and Aaron, saying, 'How long shall I bear with this evil congregation who are grumbling against Me?'" How justly God might say this of many of you today. Through the course of your lives you have grumbled against the Lord whenever anything turned out otherwise than the way you wanted it. As the verse continues, the Lord says, "I have heard the complaints of the sons of Israel." When you grumble, it may be that no one is present who hears you—except God.

The passage continues, "Say to them, 'As I live,' says the Lord, 'just as you have spoken in My hearing, so I will surely do to you; your corpses will fall in this wilderness, even all…who have grumbled against Me. Surely you shall not come into the land in which I swore to settle you." Do you feel in this God's towering indignation? It is as if he says, "As I live, this will cost you your lives!" A grumbling fit of yours, may very well cost you your life. So monitor yourself and learn to be humbled at the first onset of any such sin in your heart.

In Psalms 106: 24-26 we read: "Then they despised the pleasant land; they did not believe in His word, but grumbled in their tents; they did not listen to the voice of the Lord. Therefore He swore to them that he would cast them down in the wilderness." You see here how they slighted Gods mercies, and how they failed in faith by not believing his word. If you would only listen trustingly to the Lord, you would stop your grumbling.

These verses also demonstrate how those who lift up their hearts against God find that he lifts his hand against them. Maybe he lays his finger on you softly in some small trouble, and you grudge him this, you cannot bear it, though it lies on you as tenderly as a tender-hearted nurse lays her hand on a child. It would be no more than justice if the Lord were to lift up his hand against you with another kind of trouble. Grumbling provokes God tremendously.

70

Take a look also at Numbers 16:41: "But on the next day all the congregation of the sons of Israel grumbled against Moses and Aaron, saying, 'You are the ones who have caused the death of the Lord's people.'" Verse 46: "Moses said to Aaron, 'Take your censer and put in it fire from the altar, and lay incense on it; then bring it quickly to the congregation and make atonement for them, for wrath has gone forth from the Lord, the plague has begun!'"

Though their grumbling was against Moses and Aaron, yet since those two were God's ministers, the Israelites' complaint was indirectly against God. Perhaps you grumble against those whom God employs, his public servants, because you do not have all you want—against the Parliament or any public official. It is against God.

It is common for wicked people to thus grumble about small trials God brings them. They go on and on about it until they bring on themselves many more trials. Also pay attention to how quickly God's wrath came to the Israelites in this case. So when you are grousing and griping around home, the wrath of God may descend on you before morning has turned to evening. Friends who understand how you are setting yourself up for punishment may want to keep their distance and pray for you. You who are a godly wife, when you see your husband come home venting his discontentment, go to prayer. Say, "Lord, pardon the sin of my husband." Likewise, husband, you may need to fall on your knees and beg God to hold back his wrath that is pending against your family because of your wife's griping.

Lately there has been more grumbling in England than ever, and it is due to this that the plague has begun. Yes, God really does this to kingdoms, families, and particular persons. Though we cannot always identify the particular sin that brings it on, still we should consider how much we are guilty of the sin of grumbling.

Look also at I Corinthians 10:10, referring to the Israelites in the wilderness: "Nor grumble as some of them did, and were destroyed by the destroyer." This is thought to refer to the fiery serpents God sent among them to sting them. Do not follow the Israelites' bad example by grumbling so much about relatively slight things that God strikes you with something worse. Do not strive with your Maker! God spoke to Job out of the whirlwind and said, "Who is this that darkens counsel by words without knowledge? (Job 38:2)." Are you so bold and impudent (he said in effect) as to dare to speak against how God manages his providence?

**A great curse of God is upon wicked grumblers.**

Psalm 59:15 puts it this way: "They wander about for food and growl if they are not satisfied." The context of the verse shows this to be a curse of God on the wicked and ungodly. That is, if they are not satisfied, they will just have to 'growl' with hunger.

And in Deuteronomy 28:67 is another curse of God on the discontented. "In the morning you shall say, 'Would that it were evening!' And at evening you shall say, 'Would that it were morning!'" So they toss and turn and cannot be content for a moment with anything, because of the adversities they are enduring. Therefore, a further threat hangs over them in verse 34: "You shall be driven mad by the sight of what you see." They will be so discontented that it will drive them mad. Many people in discontented moods are half addled. Though some may please themselves with such crazy behavior, they ought to know that God curses them by abandoning them to it. They are always imagining that evils have come upon them, and they live in fear.

Verses 45-47 add, "So all these curses shall come on you and pursue you…. They shall become a sign and a wonder on you and your descendants forever. Because you did not serve the Lord your God with joy and a glad heart, for the abundance of all things; therefore you shall serve your enemies…in the lack of all things…" So this curse is for those who choose not to serve the Lord with joyfulness of heart.

**Much of Satan's spirit is in a grumbling person.**

The devil is the most discontented person in the world, the proudest and the most dejected. The more discontented you are, the more of Satan's spirit you have.

**If you are a grumbler, you will have no rest as long as you live.**

You may be like the man in a great crowd who complains that others are touching him. God has ordered things in this world so that hardships must come to us, so if we choose to complain about them, we will have to complain and be discontented every day of our lives! Quite justly, God will arrange events so as to purposely vex those who are thin-skinned about trials; and so they must always be upset. Furthermore, other people will not be careful about troubling you. Why should they if they know you will always be whining about something or other regardless?

**God may justly withdraw his care and protection from you, since you are unpleaseable.**

An employer might say to someone working for him, "If you're not happy here, find another job." Similarly, God might say to the malcontents among us, "So go find something better! If you aren't pleased with my care and protection, then try taking care of yourself!" What could be worse than to be abandoned like that? And this has actually happened to some people, so that those who know them have to say that the poor wretches live as if God had disowned them and no longer cares what happens to them.

Put that together with all the other points in this chapter, and you will see what an ugly face this sin of grumbling has. Though you used to concentrate on making a living and buying nice things, now get focused instead on humbling yourself because of your discontentedness. Let your heart break before God, because otherwise you will go right back to grumbling!

The Bible tells us how, almost inconceivably, the Israelites would go back to their grumbling over and over again. Early in Exodus 15 we find Moses and the Israelites singing praise and thanks to God for his mercy in delivering them from Egypt. But what is this? Before the chapter is over, in verses 23-24, we read, "When they came to Marah, they could not drink the waters of Marah, for they were bitter; therefore it was named Marah. So the people grumbled at Moses, saying, 'What shall we drink?'"

God gave them water, but in the very next chapter they returned to griping. Exodus 16:2-3: "The whole congregation of the sons of Israel grumbled against Moses and Aaron in the wilderness. The sons of Israel said to them, 'Would that we had died by the Lord's hand in the land of Egypt, when we sat by the pots of meat, when we ate bread to the full.'" Before they wanted water, now they want meat. God gave them meat, and not a bit ashamed of their past grumbling, they began to grumble for the lack of something else. At the beginning of chapter 17 we read that again they had no water to drink. "Therefore the people quarreled with Moses and said, 'Give us water that we may drink.' And Moses said to them, 'Why do you quarrel with me? Why do you test the Lord?' But the people thirsted there for water; and they grumbled against Moses and said, 'Why, now, have you brought us up from Egypt, to kill us and our children and our livestock with thirst?'"

So time and again they were supplied, were temporarily quieted, and were not humbled. And so it is with us. Let us be humbled before God.

## Chapter 6 - Worsening the Sin of Grumbling

Consider the following aggravations of grumbling that further demonstrate the seriousness of this sin.

### Grumbling when we enjoy many blessings

The more blessings we enjoy, the more wicked is the sin of grumbling. As we have seen, when the Israelites had just been delivered from slavery in Egypt, their grumbling due to delay in their receiving water and food was that much the worse a sin and truly abominable. Now, brethren, just this summer the Lord heaped mercies on us, one after another! Our condition is so much better than at the beginning of summer. What a mercy then that, for all our grumbling, the Lord has not punished us but has piled on the blessings instead.

We hear of blessings on our brethren in Bristol and in Scotland too. But if after this something should happen that we do not like, we would be ready at once to grumble again. What a way to thank the Lord! Instead praise him for his excellent goodness and grace.

Consider too our brethren who have risked their lives in battle for all of us. It would be an abuse of God's mercy if you decline now to help them in return, whether it be by prayer or in any other way. It would go to the heart of God. This means not letting them just shift for themselves as well as they can. That would be worsening your offence, to sin against God's mercies.

The Lord has made this summer a continuous miracle of multiplied blessings for us. Never did a kingdom enjoy such piled up mercies in so short a time. These public mercies ought to quiet our hearts and keep us from discontent about matters in our private lives. When the Lord has been so merciful to our country, will you be fretting and grumbling because your family lacks some comforts? We know that it is especially sinful for a man to gloat about his personal prosperity at a time when the public is suffering serious troubles. It is just as bad for him to be immoderately upset about his private matters when the public is rejoicing; the timing of it increases his sin.

Did you not pray for great military victories? Now that they have come to us, is that not enough to quiet your concerns about family troubles?

Someone may say to me, "That's all very well, but you don't know what we're going through. You don't feel it." I answer that, though I do not know your troubles, I know your blessings. I know they are so great that no misfortunes in the world could begin to compare to them. If we only consider that you are living another day of God's grace and salvation, that alone is greater than any misfortune. You are not now in hell: that is a great mercy. Or what about your ability to hear the gospel, to reason, and to use your limbs and your senses? Those of you who are in reasonably good health have a greater blessing than poverty is a hardship. What rich and sickly man with any sense would not part with all his money if it would buy back his health? Therefore, your mercies are greater than your misfortunes.

Consider what Moses said to Korah and his followers when they grumbled (Number 16:8-9). "Hear now, you sons of Levi, is it not enough for you that the God of Israel has separated you from the rest of the congregation of Israel, to bring you near to Himself, to do the service of the tabernacle of the Lord, and to stand before the congregation to minister to them?" No one so greatly honored by special service to God should have had any reason to grumble about any trial. So nowadays any minister of God ought not to complain about hard times and discouragements in light of all the good he is enabled to do for others.

But what about Korah and the others? The passage continues, "...and that he has brought you near, Korah, and all your brothers, sons of Levi, with you? And are you seeking for the priesthood also? Therefore you and all your company are gathered together against the Lord; but as for Aaron, who is he that you grumble against him?" They were discontent and thus intensified their sin. Learn from this, ministers of God, just to keep working for the Lord, no matter what troubles, trials, or unkindness come your way.

Another scripture we meet with is Job 2:10. His wife had counseled him to curse God and die, which we may safely say is somewhat worse than grumbling. He replied, "You speak as one of the foolish women speaks. Shall we indeed accept good from God and not accept adversity?" He shielded himself from bitter thoughts with the consideration of all the good he had had from God in his life.

Consider also Ecclesiastes 7:14: "In the day of prosperity be happy, but in the day of adversity consider—God has made the one as well as the other." Make a list of mercies and another of hardships, and see if they are not about equal. So do not focus just on the troubles: look at the other list too.

For instance, though God may have grieved you because of one child, yet he may have blessed you through another. God distressed David through his son Absalom but was merciful to him through Solomon. Similarly, if you have a good spouse, balance that against your trouble. Maybe God troubles you by loss of possessions but on the other hand gives you employment in his service. One friend is false to you while another is true. Look at both sides of the ledger and you will make God's blessings a means to lessen your sins, and not to worsen them.

Here is one more consideration. How often, regardless of our many sins, God accepts our poor duties and services. Then let us balance that, in the midst of our sufferings, by being content with whatever blessings we have.

### Grumbling about small things

In II Kings 5:13 Naaman's servant says to him, "My father, had the prophet told you to do some great thing, would you not have done it? How much more then, when he says to you, 'Wash and be clean'?" That is, Naaman was asked to do a very small thing. So if the Lord had required you, reader, to suffer through something great, would you not have been willing? How much more some small thing!

Seneca said, "Suppose a man has a very fine house with beautiful orchards and gardens, set about with handsome tall trees. Then the wind blows a few leaves off the trees. How unreasonable it would be for the man to weep and wring his hands over the loss of a few leaves when he has plenty of all kinds of fruit. So it is with many, for though they have plenty of comforts about them, yet some trivial thing will upset them." We grumble not for lack of necessities but for the lack of something extra we might possibly have. This is sinful.

Suppose God blesses a woman with a beautiful baby that is both physically and mentally perfect—except for a single wart on one finger. She wails about this: oh, what a trial it is to her! She is so consumed that she forgets to thank God for her child. Do you call that folly? Well, our own misfortunes, weighed accurately, are that light in comparison to our blessings.

It is wrong for anyone to grumble even about the worst of fates, let alone some small thing. I have read of someone who, when he lay upon a heap of damask-roses, complained because one of the rose leaves lay doubled over under him.

### Grumbling when you have gifts, abilities, and wisdom that others do not

Grumbling discontent is not allowable even for the weakest person, yet we can bear with it sometimes in children and in women who are weak. But what of men, men of understanding and wisdom whom God employs in public service? That they should be discontented with everything is evil.

### Grumbling while receiving all God's free mercies

So what if we do not have everything we want, seeing that what we do have comes as God's mercy and is free? Suppose a man were a guest in a friend's house, paying for nothing. You would not expect him to find fault with everything, would you? So it is with us who have a place at God's table daily, and all for free.

### Grumbling after receiving the things you asked for

Sometimes a child will cry for a thing, and when you give it to him, toss it aside. He is as much discontented as before. Similarly, the

Israelites cried that they must have a king, but they were not contented when they got one. As the saying goes, we are not satisfied either full or fasting.

### Grumbling after rising from poverty to success and riches

So once you said, "Oh, if God would only give me a little more wealth, I would be happy." Then God by his providence did raise you in the world, and you were still as greedy for more and as discontented. It is all too common for those who have overcome lack of education and poor beginnings to become picky and proud. These newly rich become worse than the people with 'old money.'

It is bad enough when a child is discontented in his father's house, but what if you have taken in a beggar boy who came to your door? Could you bear it that he would complain about the food and so forth? And yet you are a poor beggar, and God has, as it were, taken you into his great family. So if you have enough to live on and to be of use in the place where God has set you, will you throw a fit because you do not have everything you desire? We know that when the prodigal son in Jesus' parable came home in rags, he said, "In my father's house is bread enough." He did not say, "There is partying enough and lots of delicacies to eat." When a poor person finally gets enough simple food and a few other conveniences, commonly he wants more and better, and is still discontented.

### Grumbling after having been very sinful and ungodly

What an evil it is when people grumble who have been outrageous sinners and yet have been forgiven by God. Why not instead remind yourself that you have been guilty of shocking sins and that it is a wonder you are not now in hell? But to be discontent and grumble, how much that increases your sin!

### Grumbling when you have been of little use to others

If you have a horse that you have use of from day to day, you feed it well. But if you have little use for him, you turn him out into the

79

common grazing grounds. Little provision is enough for him because you do not make use of him. Likewise, if our consciences tell us we do little for God, then why should he not turn us out to the commons? We are being fed according to our work. Why should anything in the world serve your desires, when you do not serve God?

**Grumbling when God is about to humble you**

Suppose you have some hints that the Lord is about to humble you, to break your heart and bring you low before him. The way a Christian should walk with God is to join with him in this project. You are grumbling and discontent because of misfortune; but the very reason you are troubled is to break and humble your heart. Will you then set your will against God's? He is doing you good, if you could just see it, and if he is pleased to sanctify your hardship, to break that hard heart of yours, and to humble your proud spirit, it would be the greatest mercy you ever had in your life. To oppose him would be to say, "Well, the Lord wants to break and humble me, but I say he won't!" Though you do not use those words, it is nevertheless the language and attitude of your spirit.

**Grumbling even when God brings about your misfortune in a striking way**

When I see some extraordinary, providential events have brought hardship on me (God working overtime!), and I still grumble about it, then I sin even more. Certainly, before God's will becomes clear we may desire to avoid a hardship; but when we see God expressing his will in a remarkable way, then we ought to fall on our knees and submit to the trial. The more remarkable the events are by which God brings trouble on us, the greater is our sin in grumbling and being discontented.

I am describing a situation when God, as it were, speaks to us from heaven by name and says, "Well, I will bring down this proud spirit of yours. Don't you see that my hand is stretched out against you, my eyes and thoughts are on you, and I must bring that proud spirit down?" Then it is fitting for you to submit.

When you speak in a normal voice to your children, you expect them to obey. But when you make them come and stand by you and you speak to them in a more solemn way, then if they disregard you, you lose patience. How long do you think God's patience will last with *you*?

## Grumbling when God has been trying us for a long time

To continue your grumbling after God has been trying you for a long time is more evil than when misfortune is new to you. If a heifer continues to resist the yoke after many months or years, the farmer would rather fatten it up for the butcher and so be rid of the frustration. In the same way, though God was at first willing to wink at that discontented spirit of yours, yet after many years it would only be just for him to lower the hammer. It all may have been no more than preparation for your destruction.

You might want to underline in Hebrews 12:11 where it says, "All discipline for the moment seems not to be joyful, but sorrowful; yet to those who have been trained by it, afterwards it yields the peaceful fruit of righteousness." Of course, our hardships are hardly occasions for joy, but when you have been a long time in the school of hard knocks, you are a dimwit in Christ's classroom if you have not learned contentment. What did Paul say? "I have learned, in whatever state I am, to be content." He learned it quickly; you have been at it for many years. What an evil that you have not caught on by now! Just as the human eye becomes able to bear winter's cold, so you—even if you have a tender spirit—should have learned contentedness under hardships by now. It is shameful for veteran Christians to be grumbling.

## Chapter 7 - The Excuses of a Discontented Heart

Every malcontent has some excuse to offer. Here are the excuses, with my responses.

**'It isn't really discontent, but just awareness of my sorrows.'**

"I hope you don't expect me to be unconscious of my condition," the person says. I am referring to someone who, for example, has lost a friend or some other comfort and who goes overboard with the grieving and hand wringing, as if all were lost. But let anyone try to counsel him, and he says, "Do you want me to be emotionless?" This is the pretense some use to hide their sinful grumbling. Here is my answer:

*Mere awareness of a misfortune cannot hinder your appreciation of God's mercies.* Rather, awareness of your troubles, combined with true faith, will make you more appreciative of God's mercy. But you are so overwhelmed with negative emotion that it takes away your appreciation of his kindness. So that is the rule: if your consciousness of God's mercy is swallowed up, then you are out of bounds.

*If you were to feel no more than awareness of your sorrow, it would not hinder you from your daily duties.* But if you are unfit to work, then it must be due to more than a mere sense of your misfortune.

*If this is no more than awareness of sorrow, you should be able to thank God for the blessings others have.* Discontentedness usually breeds envy of others instead. You see them smiling and carefree and you are envious. This shows that your emotions have turned sour.

**'It's not discontent; it's concern over my sin.'**

"I'm not so much troubled by my misfortunes as by my sins," someone says, "and I do hope you will permit that we should all be troubled about our sin. If it weren't for my sins, I would not be so unhappy. Oh! It is sin that weighs on me."

Don't deceive yourself. Three considerations will show you the truth of the matter:

*You were never troubled about your sin before this misfortune came.* You will say, "True, I wasn't, because prosperity blinded me, but now God has opened my eyes by misfortunes." Has he? Then your great aim will be, of course, to get rid of your sin and not your troubles. Which do you want rid of first?

If God were to leave you in your sinfulness, but take away your troubles, would you be dissatisfied? But usually, in that case, the person does not give another thought to his sin. We see this kind of self-deception especially in those who are so distraught that they are considering suicide. Not one in ten thousand of such people is truly concerned about sin.

Recently a wise minister was visited by a man claiming to be mightily troubled by his sin, and who was ready to kill himself. The minister said, "Aren't you in debt?" The man admitted he was, and it was not long before it came out that his debt was what was really bothering him. The minister was able to help him in that matter, so that his creditors were not able to hound him so much. Once that was settled, the man calmed down and forgot all about suicide—and about sin.

How common it is, when troubles come to a man, for him to say his sins are making him miserable. Employees, when they have been called on the carpet by the boss, will be vexed and fretful. Question them, and they will say they are so sorry about their faults. But we must not play games with God, who sees right through us, searching out the secrets of our hearts.

Many of you who sullenly pace the floor at home will say it's because of your consciences. But God knows otherwise. It is because you cannot have everything the way you want it.

*If troubled by your sin, you should be extra careful not to sin in your trouble,* so as not to increase your sin. Actually, in the midst of your trouble you falsely claim to be tender about your sin, and by that wicked claim you commit more sin than you did before.

*If it is really your sin troubling you, you have greater need to submit and accept the punishment for it.* Nothing you can think of will help you so much to stop grumbling as to look upon your sin as the cause of your hardship.

### 'God has abandoned me!'

Someone wails, "How could anyone keep quiet who is abandoned by the Lord? If not for that, I hope I could be content with my misfortune. But God's presence is withdrawn from me, and that is what troubles me."

To which I answer:

*It is sheer wickedness when at every misfortune a man concludes that God has departed from him.* When the matter is examined, it may be that your only evidence of abandonment is your misfortune. In Exodus 17:7 you may see how displeased God was about such a claim. "He named the place Massah and Meribah because of the quarrel of the sons of Israel, and because they tested the Lord, saying, 'Is the Lord among us or not?'" Notice that their grievance was really about their hardship, but their *words* accused God of abandoning them. This is tempting God!

Suppose that a father corrects his son about something, and the boy wails that the father has turned into his enemy. Would that be acceptable? If you are inclined to think that God has left you desolate, I beg you to take a serious look at the passage above from Exodus.

*If God seems to have departed from you, the main reason for it is that you are so frantic and disturbed.* In other words, you are looking at it backwards. Though you are so upset, it is not because God really left you; but God has distanced himself from you because you chose to go all to pieces this way. If you would only calm down and try to be more content, then—lo and behold!—you would feel God with you again. Your emotional upheaval drives him away from you, and you cannot expect the comfort of feeling his nearness again until you have gotten a grip on yourself, while being troubled. God is only 'gone' because you are so upset.

*If you think God has left you, is your response to leave him?* Is that helpful? Well, just possibly God has left you for a while, just to try you, but if so, you hardly mend things by committing the further sin of running away from him. How brilliant! God goes from me, and I from God. If a little child sees his mother leaving him, he does not go the other way, does he? No, he goes crying after her. So my soul should say, "I see the Lord withdrawing his presence from me, so I'd better make after him with all my might. I'm sure this grumbling mood is no way to chase after God, but a way to get farther and farther away from him. What a distance will be between us before long!"

**'If I had to submit to God only, I could be content.'**

"I can bear to be in God's hands, but not in the hands of men," someone says. "When men deal so unreasonably and unjustly with me, I don't know how to bear it. It's so hard when even my friends' and acquaintances are unfair with me."

But consider these things:

*Though it is men troubling you, they are instruments of God.* They can do no more to you than he wants them to. This is what quieted King David when Shimei cursed him (II Samuel 16:5-13). "God has a hand in it," David said, in effect. "Though Shimei is a low, wicked man, yet I look beyond him to God." So do any of your friends harm and wrong you? Look up to God, and see that they are no more than tools in his hands.

*You ought to pity these people who trouble you,* rather than grumble and be discontented. For the truth is that it is better to endure being wronged by others than to do wrong yourself. They asked Socrates how he could be so patient when wronged. He replied, "If I meet a diseased man on the street, shall I be vexed by him because he is diseased? I look on those who wrong me as diseased, and so I pity them."

*Though men are cruel, you meet with nothing but kindness, goodness, and righteousness from God.* When you are wronged, balance the one against the other.

85

**'Oh, but this is a hardship that I never imagined I would meet with.'**

"The reason I'm so disturbed is that this was altogether unlooked for and unexpected."

In answer to this:

*It is your weakness and folly that you did not look for and expect it.* Consider what Paul says in Acts 20:22-23: "And now, behold, bound in spirit, I am on my way to Jerusalem, not knowing what will happen to me there, except that the Holy Spirit solemnly testifies to me in every city, saying that bonds and afflictions await me." Likewise, any Christian should expect troubles wherever he is. Though he could not have foreseen the particular evil that comes, yet it will be no more than what he looked for in general. So no misfortune should come unexpectedly to a Christian.

*So this was unexpected? The less you prepared for it beforehand, the more careful you should be now to nevertheless honor God in your heart.* Just as you should be careful to give God the glory when some mercy comes unexpectedly, so when a misfortune takes you by surprise, you should be careful to remember God and honor him. (And I may say in passing, regarding mercies, that when you moan about unexpected disaster, you ought to remember how many unexpected blessings there are as well. Set one against the other.)

We have had blessings this summer that we never expected and were unprepared for. So we should be all the more careful to give God the glory for them. Then, as regards unexpected misfortunes, well, we should have been more careful to prepare for them, and we were not. Take more pains then, in any misfortune, to thank God for his leniency.

**'Oh, but my hardship is tremendously heavy.'**

"However much you say we must be contented, you don't feel the weight of such hardship yourself, now do you? But if you felt what I do, you'd think it hard to bear contentedly."

To that I answer:

*However heavy your misfortune is, it's not as great as your sin.* God has punished you less than your sins deserve.

*It might have been much worse: you might have been in hell.* If memory serves, it was St. Bernard who said, "It is an easier matter to be oppressed than to perish."

*Maybe your hardship is so heavy because you grumble so much.* If the shoulder is sore, the burden is harder to bear. Your bad attitude makes your hardship weigh heavier on you.

**'However you try to trivialize my misfortune, I'm sure it's far worse than the burdens others bear.'**

*Maybe your discontent makes it worse, though in itself it's not so bad.*

*Supposing it to be worse, why are you so bitter when God is good to someone else?* Why should you be more discontented because God is gracious to others?

*Is your misfortune greater than others? Then you have an opportunity to honor God more than others can,* that is, by being content. Get to work on that.

*Consider that most people are worse off than you.* If your poverty is only moderate, then an equal redistribution of the world's wealth to all its inhabitants would no doubt make you not richer but *poorer*. You are above the median! Similarly, as the wise heathen Solon observed, if all the sorrows of the world were shared equally, and you had your equal share of them, your sorrows would be somewhat *increased*. Grant this, and you will have to stop claiming that your misfortunes are particularly heavy.

**'If my misfortune were only something else, I would be more contented.'**

*You must know that we are not allowed to choose the stick that God will apply to correct us.*

*It may be that, if you could exchange your misfortune for another, it would not be so suitable for you.* God may have chosen this particular burden because it is most suitable for purging out the iniquity within

87

you. A patient may say of his medicine that he could bear any other remedy than that. But it may be that no other remedy will cure his disease. If it were not so disagreeable, it would not be the cure. So your particular misfortune may be the only one that gets right at the sinfulness in your soul. God sees it as fittest and most suitable for you.

*A grace-filled Christian is fit for any condition; not just this or that, but any.* A skilled sailor does not say, "I could manage my ship if the wind blew in any direction but this." Other sailors would laugh at him, would they not? So it should be a shame for a Christian to say he has skill in any other misfortune but this. He should be able to guide his soul through any weather.

*For every situation God has a special reward for our faith*, and so allow him to reward you for this trial as well as for others.

### 'But this condition God has put me in makes me unable to serve him.'

"If this trial were a trouble to me only, that would not be so bad. But God has put me in a condition in which I can't do good for others. This is a grief to me."

If that is your grief, it is a good sign. Can you honestly say, "I count being useless in service to God as the greatest trial. I would rather bear any trouble in the world if I could be enabled to help others. I would rather do a little public service than be freed from trouble." Can you say so? If so, it is a good sign of God's grace to you.

But there may be a temptation in this, that is, if you are a poor working person lacking the free time to do public service. It is often a burden to such a person to think, 'I live in obscurity, and what purpose is there to my life?' Here are some considerations to help against this temptation, so that you will not grumble about your situation:

*Though your situation is lowly and poor, still you are in the body of believers.* Comparing this to the human body, even the toe or finger has its use, though it is not the eye, head, or heart. Or think of a tree. When a great branch of a tree is cut off, it has many leaves on it and seems far more glorious than little sprigs still on the tree. But one of those sprigs is in a better condition. Why? Because it is joined to the tree, gets sap from the root, and flourishes, but the branch will wither and die soon.

So it is with all men of the world: they are like sawn off branches. Though they are very capable and have wealth, pomp, and glory in the world, they have no union with Christ who is the root. But consider others who are lowly: a poor tradesman, a store clerk, or a laboring man. If he is godly, he may say, "Though I have little glory, credit, or comfort, still I'm joined to the Body of Christ, and so I'm supplied with what will nourish me with comfort, blessing, and mercy for all eternity." So remember that you will hold out to eternity when the glorious, pompous men will wither and perish forever, and do not be troubled about your lowly situation.

Though you are lowly in this world and do not appear to be very useful, yet being a Christian at all is the highest standing. Philippians 3:14 reads, "I press on toward the goal for the prize of the upward call of God in Christ Jesus." Every Christian has been called by God to the highest status possible. Angels in heaven do not stand higher. Even if your job is to collect garbage, your calling as a Christian advances you higher than any profession can advance anyone. Governors and billionaire businessmen are in a high calling, but yours is in some respects higher.

Though you may be mopping floors, do not moan to yourself, "Oh, what a poor condition God has put me in! Does he even care about someone as lowly as me?" Yes, Jesus does care, just as a man really cares about his toe, if it is in pain, and will look after it the same as he would his ear or his eye. So Jesus has regard for his lowliest and poorest disciples.

*You are in a high calling.* Though your occupation is lowly, in God's eyes you are in the same calling as angels. To some degree you are even higher than they, for the Bible says that it is only by observing us Christians that the angels come to understand the mystery of the gospel. Just by being a Christian, you are joined with archangels and angels in the greatest work of God. So take comfort in this.

*If you are godly, you have a grace of God in you which raises your lowest actions higher than all the brave, glorious actions done in the world.* The principle of faith does it. Your faithful obedience in a lowly situation makes your activities more glorious than all the battlefield victories of Alexander and Caesar.

Also, it is more obedient to submit to God in a lowly job than in a prestigious one. This is because it is obedience alone that makes you go on working at a low wage, but those with prestigious professions have additional motives of self-love, such as riches, honor, and fame. To go on quietly in a lowly job is more obedient to God.

*There is likely to be more reward for you.* When the Lord comes to reward, he does not examine what work people have done, but how faithful they have been. We can all quote God's words, "Well done, good and faithful slave (Matthew 25:21)." He does not say, "Well done, good servant, for you have been faithful to me in public works, ruling cities and states, and affairs in kingdoms, and therefore you shall be rewarded."

You may be just as faithful in a little as others are in a lot. When you keep on with the daily grind, and pull in a few pounds to support your family, you may be as faithful as those who rule a kingdom. God looks to faithfulness, and so you may have as great a reward from working in a restaurant kitchen all day as another who sits on a throne. Then why should not every one of us go on comfortably and cheerfully in our low condition, for might we not be as faithful as those who are rich and honored? Yes, you may have a glorious crown in heaven, and therefore go on securely and happily in your path.

**'Oh, I could bear trouble in some other way, but my condition is so unsettled and unpredictable!'**

"However lowly I might end up, if only matters were settled, I could be content. But my situation is so inconstant that I never know what to trust in. I'm tossed up and down in the world."

To this I answer:

*Psalm 39:5 says that "every man at his best is a mere breath,"* and 'at his best' should be translated 'in his settled estate.' You think, if your affairs were settled, that you would be content, but the truth is, man in his settled estate is a mere breath.

*Perhaps God knows it is better for you to live in continual dependence on him,* not knowing what tomorrow will bring, than for you to be settled in worldly comforts. Remember what I wrote before, that Jesus teaches us to pray for just today's bread, not a year's supply. This is to teach us to rely on him for our daily needs.

In the Bible the land of Canaan depended on God for rain, but Egypt had the seasonal flooding of the Nile to water it. That predictable river water made the Egyptians grow proud. The Bible even quotes Pharaoh as saying, "My Nile is mine (Ezekiel 29:3)." God thought Canaan, with its unpredictable rain, was a better land for his people than Egypt, because there they would depend on him. So godly people who do not know how they will pay next month's rent apply more faith than some others and are in a better condition in their souls. Often we can say that the worse off you are financially, the better your soul is; and the better off you are financially, the worse your soul is.

Read in Ezra 4:13 the objection that Israel's enemies made to their rebuilding the wall around Jerusalem. They wrote to King Ataxerxes against the Jews, saying, "Now let it be known to the king that if that city is rebuilt and the walls are finished, they will not pay tribute, custom, or toll, and it will damage the revenue of the kings." As soon as they would be able to defend themselves from behind stout walls, it would be all over between them and the King. That is just how it is between God and men's souls. While our affairs are in flux and we see everything depends on God, we pay toll and custom to him in the form of faith, begging him every day for our bread. But let God hedge a man about with prosperity—maybe by an inheritance or a good steady job—and his prayer falls off. We all want to be independently wealthy, and wave goodby to God, but he sees it is better for us to lean on him.

Take comfort that, though your outward life is precariously unsettled, yet the great things of your soul and eternal welfare are firmly established. For one thing, you have a settled source of supply: "For of his fullness we have all received, and grace upon grace (John 1:16)." So you have an abundant treasure to go to and get all you need. And better that the treasure should be firmly in God's hands than in yours! He keeps it safely.

**"If I had never known prosperity, then I could bear this misfortune.'**

Perhaps a man has had a very good annual income that has now been cut off. Let us say that he still has some money and has friends willing to help him. What troubles him most, he says, is that he was once in a better condition. But this is unreasonable of him: *Are you bitter because God was so good to you before?* It is bad enough for you to be bitterly envious of others God has blessed, but to be bitter because God blessed *you!* Has God done you any wrong by having once favored you more than he did others?

*If God gave you more prosperity before, it was to prepare you for troubles.* If you had used that time of prosperity to prepare for troubles, it would not be so hard on you now. Every Christian should say, "Am I wealthy now? I should prepare for poverty. Am I healthy? I should prepare for sickness. Am I free? Let me prepare myself for imprisonment. How do I know what God may call me to? If my conscience is clear now, with God shining on me, let me prepare for his withdrawing from me. Am I delivered from temptations? Let me prepare for a season of temptations."

If you would think like that, the coming changes would not be so hard on you. If the weather has been calm then prepare for a storm, like any good sailor, and the storm that comes will be less damaging.

Your reasoning should be just the opposite of what it is. Say, "I'm troubled now, but I thank God that he strengthened me beforehand with so many blessings." And also this, "I lived for decades in health, peace, and plenty. What of it if I spend my last years in some sorrow and hardship? My life has been a day of sunshine until evening, so what if at seven or eight o'clock at night it begins to rain? Let me thank God for the beautiful day I've had."

Or suppose you have been on a year's voyage and encounter a little storm when in sight of your home shore? Will you grumble? Rather, thank God that you have had a comfortable voyage for so long.

Suppose God were to say to you, "Well, you'll never see comfortable days again in this world." You have cause then to fall down on your knees and honor him because you have had so many comfortable days. But you actually want to make your former comforts a reason to feel worse!

On what legal terms did you hold the comforts you had before? Did you have in your legal documents the phrase, 'To have and to hold forever'? God gives no such thing. God gives no man anything but grace to last the terms of the lease. If he gives me an understanding of himself; and if he give me faith, humility, love, patience, and other such graces of the Spirit; he gives me those things forever. If he gives me himself, Christ, his promises, and his covenant, he gives me those too forever. But when it comes to worldly comforts, who am I that the sun should always shine on me, that I am entitled to fair weather all my life?

Rather, any worldly comforts a godly man receives from God are a pledge of God's love for him. Therefore, when he meets with troubles, it is God saying to him, "I gave you blessings as a pledge of my love. Return them to me as a pledge of your obedience." We should cheerfully do it and thank God that we have anything to return to him, saying, "It's your love, Lord, which has given us everything, which enables us to return a pledge of our obedience to you."

**'To be thwarted now, after I have taken a great deal of pains to get this comfort, oh, it is very hard.'**

*The greater the misfortune, the more you should obey and submit.*

*While you were taking such great pains, were you submitting to God?* Or were you resolved that you *must* have the thing you worked so hard for? Then you did not labor as a Christian. You should have labored with inner resignation to God, saying, "Lord, I am working hard in my profession, but with submission to you; I depend wholly on you for success and a blessing." And what was your goal in your labor? Was it that you might walk obediently with God in the situation he put you in? Your diligence at your job should be your way of obeying him. "It's true that I'm providing for my family," you may say, "but the main thing is that I obey the Lord where he has placed me."

Therefore, if God calls you to obey him in some other situation, then even if it involves suffering, you will do it if your heart is right.

*It better demonstrates your love for God if you submit to him in what cost you so dearly.* King David did not want to offer to God

93

anything that had cost him nothing (II Samuel 24:24). By submitting to losing what cost you so much, you offer up to God something of real value.

### 'I don't flare up into expressions of discontent.'

Some say, "I thank God that I keep my discontent bottled up, although I feel it keenly in my heart." But do not satisfy yourself with that, because to God the thoughts of your heart are the same as spoken words. Let both your tongue and your soul be silent. Unless you mortify that sullen discontentedness in your heart, when the misfortune gets a little worse your tongue will break loose sharply enough.

I implore you, in the name of God, to consider all the above answers and remember them.

## Chapter 8 - How to Achieve Contentment

# How to be contented in any condition

*Consider the greatness of the blessings you have and the littleness of the things you lack.* For the most part the things you lack (and grumble about lacking) are the same sort of things that godless people have, or may have. Why have a fit over something that a godless person may have? So what if your bank account is small, your health indifferent, or your credit rating low? You might have had both health and wealth and still have been a faithless person.

Anthony meets blind Daniel on the street and asks, "Daniel, aren't you troubled about being blind?"

Daniel replies, "Sure, but should a person be troubled about not having what flies and dogs have? Shouldn't I rejoice and be thankful that I do have what angels have?"

God has given you the good things that make angels glorious, and is that not enough for you? "Blessed be the God and Father of our Lord Jesus Christ," the Apostle Paul says in Ephesians 1:3, "who has blessed us with every spiritual blessing in the heavenly places..." Regardless of how little you have on earth, if the Lord has blessed you spiritually 'in heavenly places,' that ought to content you.

*Consider all the mercies God has given you already.* You have had mercy enough already to prompt you to spend the rest of your days thanking God. I once read of a fifty year old man who had been healthy forty-eight years, but for the last two years had experienced severe pain in urinating. He reasoned it out to himself like this: "It's good to consider that God has supplied us so much mercy in the past.

Instead of fixating on how much worse off we are, we should thank God for what we have had. We might have been miserable every day since birth!"

*Consider the abundance of mercies we enjoy.* Martin Luther said, "The sea of God's mercies should swallow up all our particular afflictions." Name anything that troubles you and there is a sea of mercy to swallow it up. If you pour out a bucket of water on the floor of your house, it is rather startling, but if you throw it in the sea, there is no sign of it. So if you focus on troubles, they seem important, but if you consider them in the context of God's sea of mercies, they shrink to insignificance.

*Consider the way of God towards all creation.* God makes everything vary as time passes. Winter succeeds summer and night succeeds day. Foul weather follows fair. Trees flourish and then become dormant for months. If God orders all other things in cycles, why should we think it such an affront that he at times gives us prosperity and at other times misfortune?

*Created things suffer for us; why should we not be willing to suffer in order to serve God?* In the *Book of Martyrs*, Master Hooper said that he had observed how creatures suffered for him. Beasts, for example, are killed, roasted, put on a dinner plate, hacked to pieces, chewed, and digested—and all to nourish us. He asked why he, then, should not be willing to be made into anything for God's service? If God would impoverish him, take away his life, hack him in pieces, put him in prison—whatever—yet he ought to suffer more for God than creatures suffer for him. "And surely," he concluded, "I am infinitely more bound to God than the creatures are to me, and creatures are not so far below me as I am below God!"

Such consideration helped this martyr to be content in his sufferings.

*Consider that we have just a short time in this world.* If you are godly, you will never suffer except in this world. As a martyr said to his companion martyr, "Just shut your eyes, and the next time they are opened you shall be in another world." When Athanasius was banished, he said, "It is but a little cloud and it will be over, notwithstanding, soon." These hardships are but for a moment. When a sailor at sea can see clear skies beyond the present storm, he says, "It will be over soon." You do not have long to live, and the hardship may end before you die. But supposing it does not, death will put an end to all troubles.

*Consider the sufferings of those who were better people than we are.* The Patriarch Jacob, who was heir to Abraham and to God's blessing and promise, lived nevertheless for quite a few years as a poor man. Moses, who might have had all the treasure of Egypt, lived forty years as a shepherd. Afterwards, when he returned to Egypt with his wife and children, he had only one donkey for transportation.

The prophet Elijah was fed by ravens and had to flee for his life from time to time. Many of God's prophets were hidden in a cave by Obadiah, and there fed with bread and water. Jeremiah was put in a dungeon and treated terribly there. It would be endless to name all the particulars of how God's people have suffered.

We could consider also those who suffered during the first Reformation. Martin Luther himself, when he was about to die, said, "Lord, I have neither house, nor lands, nor estate, to leave anything to wife and children, but I commit them to thee." Musculus, who was worth a kingdom due to his excellence of spirit and his scholarship, was reduced to digging ditches to get bread for his family. Would you trade places with him?

Above all, let us set Christ before us, who had no place to lay his head.

It is also useful for wealthy folk to visit poor people's houses, hospitals, and alms houses, to see how plain their food is and how pitifully they have declined in the world. Hearing about it is one thing, but if you could see them, it would not only stir up charity in you but also thankfulness to God, and it would suppress your discontentedness. You would go away saying, "If I were in their place, what would I do? How could I bear it? And yet why has God made them so lowly and raised me up? I know of no reason but free grace: he has mercy on whom he wishes."

Such thoughts are strong cures for discontentment.

*Before your conversion you used to be contented to have the things of the world and no grace; why not be contented now with grace and spiritual things but without the world?* You see that many men of the world have a kind of contentment. Then why not be at least as content with God and Christ? Otherwise it would be shameful.

97

*Consider the times when God has given you your heart's desire, and you did not give him the glory.* Consider too the times when you got your heart's desire and have been no better for it, perhaps even worse.

*Consider all the good God has brought to you even in the midst of hardships.* When a preacher says God will bring good out of your misfortunes, you listen politely, feeling that it is just the way church people talk, and you do not feel the good, but only pain. But what if I say to you that you yourself have found it so by experience? Because surely you must admit that God has made former trials turn to your benefit, and that you would not for the world have missed them and the good that came with them. So if it has happened in the past, why not again? Such reflections quiet the heart and bring it to contentment.

I will add just one more thing. Once a great merchant and trader named Zeno suffered shipwreck. He said later, "I never made a better voyage and sailed better than at the time I suffered shipwreck." By this paradoxical statement he meant that God had made him richer in his soul because of this disaster.

You too may have found that your worst voyages were your best. When God in his providence orders things so that you meet with bad times, you have learned to expect that he will turn them to a greater good. If you have been a Christian for many years, you no doubt have many such stories to tell.

In a storm at sea a small ship can slip into some shallow place and be safe, but large ships cannot and must be tossed up and down in the tempest and many times split against the rocks. Well, God has put you, Christian, in a smaller vessel so you can be safe.

**How to direct your heart to achieve contentment**

*All the rules and advice in the world will do us little good unless we get a good attitude.* You can never make a ship go steady by propping it outside; you know there must be ballast within the ship to make it go steady. And so there is nothing outside us that can keep our hearts steady and constant, but rather what is within us: grace within the soul will do this.

*If you are to have a contented life, do not grasp too much of the world.* Do not take on more business than God calls you to. If you do,

98

you will be like a man going through thorn bushes when he might have taken a clear path. He has no reason to complain about scratches, does he? If you must necessarily go among thorn bushes, then that is another matter, but if you choose the thorny way when you might have taken another, do not complain.

The world's nature is such that everything in it has some tendency to scratch us. We will meet with disappointments in everything we get involved with, and therefore the less we have to do with the world, the more satisfaction.

*Be sure you are called by God to every business you take on.* Even if it is a small matter, be sure of your call to it. Then, whatever the result, you may quiet your heart with this: "I'm where God wants me to be. I'm doing the work God has assigned me." The Lord will watch over you and see that you are blessed if you are working at what he has called you to.

*Follow the rules of the work you are called to.* You must be guided by the Bible and discipline yourself in your work according to God's views as much as possible. Put this together with the last point, about being sure of God's call, and you have an unbeatable combination. Your quiet and peace will be perfect. Whatever may come, God will take care of you.

The reason why many of our gentry are able to behave so hatefully toward us is that they are first willing to be slaves themselves under those above them at the King's Court. They submit to be slaves in order that they can keep their neighbors under, to be slaves to them. For you know how it used to be that any man notable in Court had the influence to crush any countryman of his that he was angry with. In an arbitrary government, anyone willing to be a vassal and slave to the Prince can make all others vassals and slaves under him.

Now be willing to be a vassal to God, to be absolutely under his command, and all things in the world will be under you. All things serve someone who is in God's service. What a strong recommendation to serve him! Though you do not command events yourself, God arranges them all to work for your good.

So long as we stay in our bounds, we are under protection, but if we step out we will be like deer straying outside a park. While they stay in the park, no dog hunts them and they can feed quietly, but let them go outside and every dog in the county will be after them. So it is with us. Let us stay within the bounds of the rules God has set for us in the Bible, and we are protected by him. We may go about our business in peace, never troubled by anything, but casting all our care on him. God provides for us. But if we go beyond our bounds, we may expect to meet with troubles, trials, and discontent. Do go by the rules.

*Apply great faith.* After you have considered everything that commends itself to your reason, if it does not seem enough, then call for the grace of faith. You can go far on reason, but when reason is baffled, set faith to work. The reverend divine Master Perkins said, "The life of faith is a true life, indeed the only life." Believe not only that all will work together for good for those who fear God, but also put your faith in God's attributes: his love, his perfect knowledge, his power, and so forth. Socrates, though a heathen, said, "Since God is so careful of you, what need you be careful for anything yourselves?"

Christian, if you have any faith, then in time of crisis remember: this is the time to use that faith of yours. What use is faith if you cannot quiet your discontentment?

Dionysius had been a king, and afterwards was reduced to the level of schoolmaster. Someone visited him and asked, "What have you gotten from your philosophy of Plato and others?"

"I've got this," he said, "that though I've fallen so low in my situation, yet I can be content."

So, Christian, what have you gotten from being a believer? What can you do by faith? You can in every circumstance give up your worries to God and commit your paths to him in peace. Faith can do this.

Therefore, when reason can climb no higher, let faith get on reason's shoulders and say to reason, "I see our destination, though you can't see it. I see good that will come out of all this evil." Apply faith by often resigning yourself to God's will, by giving yourself up to him and his ways. The more you do that, the more peace you will have.

*Labor to be spiritually minded.* Often meditate on spiritual things. The reason we are so troubled by our blocked desires is that we talk too little with God. Focusing on spiritual things would lift us above the things of the world.

You will not be bitten by a snake unless you walk on the ground. If you could be lifted above the earth, you would never be bitten. Grumbling, and the temptations and evils that accompany it, are like snakes that crawl the earth. If we could get higher we would not be bitten by them. Communion with heaven is the way to contentment.

*Do not promise yourself too much beforehand.* Do not aim too high in your thoughts, thinking, "Oh, if I had such and such!" You could get lost in imagining marvelous things. Instead be as good as Jacob who asked the Lord to just "give me food to eat and garments to wear (Genesis 28:20)." He looked no higher and was content. So if we would stop trying to keep up with the Joneses, we would not be so crushed by disappointments.

On the other hand, soar as high as you wish in spiritual meditations. God gives you liberty there to go as high as you want, even above angels. But for your outward status, God does not want you to aim at high things. In these times especially, it would be evil for anyone to aim for greatness. Do not seek for great things. Be willing to creep low, and if God raises you up, you will have cause to thank him. But if you are not raised, you do not risk much trouble. He who creeps low cannot fall far, but it is the one high up who is bruised most by a fall.

*Labor to make your heart dead to the world.* Thinking about the vanity of worldly things is not enough. We must go beyond that to apply self-mortification and to be crucified to the world. The Apostle Paul said, "I die daily (I Corinthians 15:31)." So should we. When the scripture says that we are baptized into the death of Jesus Christ (Romans 6:3), it signifies that we claim to be like men dead to the world. Now no trials of this world trouble those who are dead. If our hearts were dead to the world, we would not be much troubled with the world's ups and downs; nothing would bother us much.

So what does 'dead to the world' mean? It is to have our hearts drawn away from the things of the world, so that we use them as if we did not use them, not accounting that our lives, comforts, and happiness consist in such things. Our happiness consists in things of a different kind. When we can be happy without the things of the world, that is a kind of deadness to the world.

101

_Do not be preoccupied with your troubles._ That is, do not busy your thoughts too much with brooding over your misfortunes. You find many people whose every thought is taken up with their troubles, so they do nothing but think and talk about them. It is the first thing they think of when they wake at night and the first thing they speak of when they meet you on the street. Perhaps even when they are praying they are thinking of their misfortunes. Is it any wonder that you live a discontented life if you are always poring over your troubles? Instead try to turn your thoughts to things that comfort you.

Many people, if you give them spiritual advice that will help them stop such brooding, will take it well in your presence, and thank you for it; but once they are out the door, they soon forget it.

Jacob's wife wanted to name her son Benoni, that is, 'son of sorrows.' Jacob wisely called him Benjamin instead, which means 'son of my right hand.' Thus, his son always reminded him of something cheerful instead of sorrows.

Basil, a learned man, said that those with sore eyes should not strain them by looking at bright lights, such as a fire, but instead should look at soothing things. So it is with those with weak spirits. Do not look into the fire of your misfortunes, at dejecting and depressing things, but concentrate on matters suitable to heal and help you.

_Put a positive interpretation on what happens to you._ If any good interpretation can be made of God's ways towards you, make it. You are irritated if some friend constantly misinterprets whatever you say or do, putting a bad face on it. You can hardly get a word out in conversation before some people are taking it wrongly. But it is likewise tedious to God when we take wrongly his ways toward us. If one sense worse than another can be put on it, we are sure to do it.

So when you face a hardship, and any number of interpretations can be put on it, choose a good one. Say to yourself, "Maybe God intends to try me by this. Maybe God saw my heart was too much set on the things of this world, and so he intends to hold up a mirror to me. Or maybe God saw that if I were to continue so wealthy, I would have fallen into sin; and the better my worldly standing, the worse off my soul. Or God may intend to build my faith, or to prepare me for some good work."

Instead we tend to say, "God is mad at me. This is just the beginning of more miseries he intends for me. He wants me dead."

102

We forget that the Bible says that love thinks no evil. So if there are ten interpretations to be put on a misfortune, nine bad and one good, you ought to choose the good one and let the others drop.

Contrast how God interprets *your* actions. If he were to pick the worst interpretation of your ways toward him, you would be in a world of trouble. Rather he is pleased to choose an explanation of our actions that is improbable. For example, he is pleased to call those perfect who have any uprightness of heart in them. And also, when we look into our hearts, we see uncleanness, but for all that, God calls us saints. He lists under the name of saint any corrupt Christian who has the least grace. If there is a lot of evil and a little good, God passes over the evil and notices the good.

Abraham's wife Sarah once made a bad and unbelieving speech to him (Genesis 18:12) in which she addressed him as her 'lord'—one good word out of the lot. But when the Apostle Peter mentioned that speech in I Peter 3:6, the Holy Spirit led him to leave out all the bad and commend her for calling her husband her lord, for putting a reverent title on him. How graciously God deals with us!

Brethren, be like that toward the Lord. Keep good thoughts of God. Do not call him a hard master but make good interpretations of what he does. That is a special way to arrive at contentment.

*Do not regard the opinions of others as much as your own.* This is because we often become discontented more because of what others say than because of what we ourselves feel. For example, the reason we think poverty is such a great evil is that others tell us so. Poor people do not necessarily think it is all that bad, unless they are in extremes.

You may think your wealth is small, but if everyone in the world were even poorer than you, far from being discontented, you would rejoice. Were it not for the disgrace, disregard, and snubs of others, you might feel happy and content.

*Do not get carried away with the luxuries of this world.* When you have them, do not be overly satisfied with them. It is a certain rule: to the degree a man is excessive in sorrow after losing some comforts, he was just that excessive in rejoicing when he had them. For instance, God takes a child from you and your grief is excessive, beyond what God allows in a natural or Christian way. Even though you may be a

103

stranger to me, I may reasonably conclude that you had set your heart immoderately on that child before it died. If you hear of a stock market plunge, and are immoderately depressed, certainly you had already been infatuated with your stock portfolio. So also with your reputation. If you overhear others gossiping venomously about you, and your heart sinks, then you must have already been overly concerned about your good name.

Clearly, the way to avoid excessive sorrow about adversity is not to be so giddy when you have prosperity.

To conclude, if I were to tell you I had a formula to keep you from ever lacking anything you want, and that I would preach about it on Sunday morning, then doubtless it would be standing room only. But what I have written amounts to the same thing. Is it not practically the same, never to lack anything, or never to be without contentment? Whoever is always content cannot be said to lack much.

The Bible shows us the way of comfort and peace even in this world. You may live a happy life in the midst of storms and tempests. Enter this ark and no man in the world may live as comfortably, cheerfully, and contentedly as you.

Though I have filled a book with this lesson, I am afraid that you will be longer in learning it than you were in reading it. Many who for many years have claimed to be Christians have hardly begun on it. If you are a young Christian, you had better start early! Many Christians are struggling with this every day of their lives and still are not capable. But God forbid that any of us should be on a sort of treadmill, never advancing. A sailor with twenty years' experience at sea would be shamed if he had achieved no skill in navigation. Do not let it be said that you who have been Christians for twenty years have achieved no skill in contentment. Do not be content with yourselves until you have learned this lesson of Christian contentment.

## About Rob Summers

Rob Summers is an author of indie novels that reflect his Christian faith. He lives with his wife in a small house on six wooded acres in rural Indiana. Besides enjoying writing, he plays chess and strums guitar chords.

Rob Summers' books are available for purchase in multiple ebook formats, through Amazon's Kindle Store and other ebook retailers. You may want to visit Rob Summers' Amazon author page at www.amazon.com/author/robsummers%20 to read a sample or to purchase for your Kindle reader.

His email is robsummers76@gmail.com. He welcomes your comments or questions.

Made in the USA
Columbia, SC
19 December 2019